# Identifying and Supporting Children with Specific Learning Difficulties

How do you deal with the challenge of teaching children with specific learning difficulties?

Many children experience difficulties which impact on their learning at home and school. Some children are considered to have a specific learning difficulty such as dyslexia or dyspraxia, but other children display a range of indicators which cross the boundaries of specific named 'conditions'. If teachers are to offer appropriate support, the authors of this highly practical book argue that they must look beyond the label to assess the whole child.

This informative book,

- encourages teachers to consider children as individuals rather than attempting to match them to existing sets of indicators
- pinpoints the overlap of indicators within different specific learning difficulties
- considers the process of assessment
- explains the implications of the children's difficulties
- offers tried and tested strategies to promote inclusive learning.

Teachers, teaching assistants, SEN coordinators and students undertaking teacher training courses will all find this a refreshingly accessible book.

**Dr Christine Macintyre** and **Pamela Deponio** teach in the Moray House School of Education at the University of Edinburgh.

# Identifying and Supporting Children with Specific Learning Difficulties

## Looking beyond the label to assess the whole child

## Christine Macintyre and Pamela Deponio

RoutledgeFalmer
Taylor & Francis Group

LONDON AND NEW YORK

First published 2003
by RoutledgeFalmer
11 New Fetter Lane, London EC4P 4EE

Simultaneously published in the USA and Canada
by RoutledgeFalmer
29 West 35th Street, New York, NY 10001

*RoutledgeFalmer is an imprint of the Taylor & Francis Group*

© 2003 Christine Macintyre and Pamela Deponio

Typeset in Times by
HWA Text and Data Management, Tunbridge Wells
Printed and bound in Great Britain by
TJ International, Padstow, Cornwall

*British Library Cataloguing in Publication Data*
A catalogue record for this book is available from the British Library

*Library of Congress Cataloging in Publication Data*
A catalog record for this book has been requested

ISBN 0–415–31494–1 (hbk)
ISBN 0–415–31495–X (pbk)

# Contents

# Illustrations

## Figures

## Tables

# Acknowledgements

There are many people who have contributed to the completion of this book and we offer a huge thank you to them all. First to the parents and children who have shared their hopes and dreams, their pleasures when these were fulfilled and their disappointments when progress took longer than planned. They were all so generous in giving us the benefit of their experiences, in telling us ways that worked best and those which did not encourage their children to persevere.

Second to the teachers who 'looked beyond the label' and began to question the assessments their children had. Despite a time of 'not being sure' because they had always relied on labels to tell them what was amiss, they now consider that 'a wider look' is critically important. This results in the children being assessed in each aspect of development with their strengths being recorded as well as their areas of need. In this way the children can be assessed as themselves, not as people made to 'fit' the criteria describing a specific learning difficulty. The assessments can then form the basis of the most appropriate individual action plan.

And lastly to the excellent secretarial duo at Edinburgh University, Moira Avraam and Lorraine Dodds. They were unfailingly cheerful and helpful and had all the answers as to why our computers 'didn't work'! Their skill in producing the artwork for the book is very much appreciated.

Thank you to you all.

# Chapter 1

# Raising the issues

## An overview

In the opening years of the twenty-first century, there has been an astounding 80 per cent increase in the number of children who are being identified as having a specific difficulty which hinders their learning (Keen 2001). This means that there will be children with these difficulties in every class. Members of staff therefore have to understand both the distinctive aspects of and the considerable overlap between each specific learning difficulty. While there are many such difficulties, the ones considered in this book are dyslexia, dyspraxia, the attention deficit disorders (ADD), or with the added hyperactivity (ADHD), Asperger's syndrome, specific language impairment (SLI) and the Scandinavian-named DAMP (deficit in attention, motor control and perception). 'Specific learning difficulties' is an umbrella term which indicates that children display discrepancies across their learning, exhibiting areas of high competence alongside areas of significant difficulty.

Whether in reality there are more children than ever before or whether parents and other professionals are more aware of the symptoms which indicate that problems may be looming and are more anxious to push for diagnosis and help is a moot point; but 'more children' there certainly are, to the extent that physiotherapists, occupational therapists and psychologists say they cannot cope with the increased demand on their services. Certainly in schools, teachers find that the number of possible referrals is very limited and waiting times to see specialists are unacceptably long. To offset this and to try to ensure that all children are enabled to fulfil their potential and make the most of their time in school, teachers are being urged to make a comprehensive assessment of children's difficulties. This includes evaluating the strategies they put in place to help them, e.g. reflecting critically on any learning materials which have been adapted to meet the children's needs.

Many caring professionals would claim that they are doing much of this already, for they are constantly on the look out for difficulties as a natural part of their teaching and supporting the children. When these appear, they consult the support for learning staff or SENCOs (special educational needs coordinators), plan the most appropriate learning materials together and then monitor the children's progress. Others, however, claim that this seemingly ideal cooperation just can't happen. They explain that with the best will in the world, 'it's almost impossible to find time to understand all the complexities of each specific learning difficulty and prepare differentiated work for children, taking into account their different levels of physical, intellectual, social and/or emotional difficulty'. Many blame the priority given to 'getting children to meet the [externally imposed] targets' and find that teaching to meet this outcome results in other important aspects of education having to go on the back burner! Nursery staff often feel particularly aggrieved that they have no in-house experts to help them identify difficulties. At a critically important time, when early intervention could be particularly effective and when some difficulties could be ameliorated before the children were even aware that they had them, these professionals have to cope alone. Across the board something has to be done.

The premise of this book is that there are common features within specific learning difficulties and that understanding these will also show how the children can be helped in groups. This would prevent feelings of isolation, even 'being picked on' which children describe and reduce the amount of differentiated planning which would need to happen if each child was supported individually. This sounds ideal ... but what evidence is there to show that this overlap exists? In Canada, Kaplan *et al.* (2001) present data from a study of 179 school age children assessed for seven disorders: reading disability (dyslexia), developmental coordination disorder (dyspraxia), attention deficit disorder (ADD) with the addition of hyperactivity (ADHD), conduct disorders, depression and anxiety. They discovered that 'fully 50 per cent of the sample met the criteria for at least two of the diagnoses', and also claimed that 'children with ADHD were at a higher risk of having a second disorder'. As the numbers of children with difficulties are increasing so that there may be several in each class, this book offers parents and teaching staff help in identifying children with difficulties, in understanding their symptoms and in designing strategies to facilitate teaching and learning. In the ethos of an inclusive culture, it

- highlights the overlap of difficulties within different special needs conditions
- considers the process of assessment
- explains the source and the implications of these difficulties
- lists tried and tested strategies to help the children, their parents and the school professionals cope
- confirms that these steps complement the new inclusive policies.

This information means that parents and children can be reassured that new, inclusive ways are evolving and that a greater understanding of children's difficulties will lead to them being given the most appropriate help for the correct length of time.

In the past, children who did not match some hypothetical 'norm' were often simply urged to cope as best they could. There was one lesson for all, albeit with some extension work for the 'able' ones and some less challenging work for those needing more practice. Very often this resulted in the latter group believing they were stupid or inadequate, when indeed the education system had made no real provision for their difficulties. Trying to make the children match the norm, teachers often concentrated on the things the children could not do – to little avail – and failed to recognize and develop the competencies the children had. It is no wonder that many children and adults floundered and eventually rejected a system which saw them as failures. Children with the most severe difficulties were educated in special schools where specially trained teachers understood and managed their problems and where the more favourable teacher:child ratio allowed for individualized care. But then the children were seen as 'different' and they missed out on opportunities for social interaction which is such an important part of development. Neither could they benefit intellectually from sharing lessons with their peers and so their difficulties were compounded by the very arrangements which had been designed to help them.

The policy of inclusion means that this should no longer happen, and while this is very good news, there is much progress still to be made. There are many unanswered questions about ways to make inclusion 'work' in a culture of meeting targets and gaining a high place in league tables – goals which do not appear to consider that all aspects of the children's education are of equal importance. There are conflicting pieces of advice as to what to do and how to do it and many theories still to be evaluated in terms of realistically making them work in schools. Much rests on the debate as to what education in school is for and the place competencies like 'compassion' and 'empathy' have in the value system that drives the ethos of the school.

Why should there be confusion and even conflict when everyone has the same goal, i.e. to understand the children's difficulties and to develop strategies to overcome/circumvent them? There are several reasons why:

- the large number of children who have to be assessed
- the correspondingly large number of assessors involved
- the pressure these assessors feel in 'having' to give a diagnosis in case children are subsequently denied individual programmes of help
- the overlap of symptoms making assessments complex
- the fact that there are different levels of impairment and that children's competence may fluctuate, making accurate assessment problematic.

The sheer number of children presenting with specific difficulties means that different groups of professionals are making assessments and advising what is to be done. Their own professional training is likely to have concentrated on different aspects of the children's development, so this may cause them to focus on things which are familiar to them. The overlap of key indicators means they are likely to identify these before 'the whole child' has been assessed. Classroom teachers are likely to focus on the skills of reading, spelling, talking and writing because developing these fundamental and pervasive skills is an important part of their initial training. And so, when children find these areas difficult, the teachers may well diagnose dyslexia (Croll and Moses 1985), missing the possibility of SLI (specific language impairment). On the other hand, teachers of physical education, physiotherapists and occupational therapists, trained in the observation of perception and movement, may first consider dyspraxia because they have focussed on the practical, 'being able to do' side of things and they know that competent movement underlies much learning. Moreover, they know that they have the expertise to help poor coordination, balance and any movement difficulty, which impacts on the children's learning.

And what of psychologists and/or psychotherapists who have studied behaviour difficulties? Perhaps when they see children who can't pay attention or concentrate, they will most readily suspect ADD (attention deficit disorder) or, if constant movement is a key disabling factor, ADHD (attention deficit hyperactivity disorder). Again these are competencies which strongly impact on the ability to learn, for children who disrupt others, by moving around, interrupting inappropriately or being aggressive, may soon find that they are rejected and blamed even for things they did not do. Yet this inability to sit still and concentrate may have been caused by poor muscle tone which affected the children's balance or they may have poor body awareness and need continuous tactile feedback to let them know where they are functioning in space. These children need help for these specific competencies. They may not have ADHD at all. Farnham-Diggory (1992) claims that 80 per cent of children are misclassified. This is a very frightening statistic.

This being the case, i.e. that different experts concentrate on different aspects of the children's behaviour (see Figure 1.1), it is not difficult to understand the perplexity and bewilderment of parents who discover that *other* children, with ostensibly the same difficulties as their own, have been given a different diagnosis. They are left in a quandary, wondering who is right. The whole child must be assessed.

## How can this confusion arise?

### Case study 1

Listen to Gayle, Leah's mum, talking about her daughter who is eight years old and 'totally miserable at school'. Gayle 'is at her wits' end' and has had several interviews with professionals at school which were helpful but still haven't resolved the problem. She explains,

> Leah is a fragile, dainty child, very pretty but rarely smiling. She appears to cooperate with anything she's asked to do but she never finishes a job and never seems to realize that this is unacceptable. She avoids getting involved

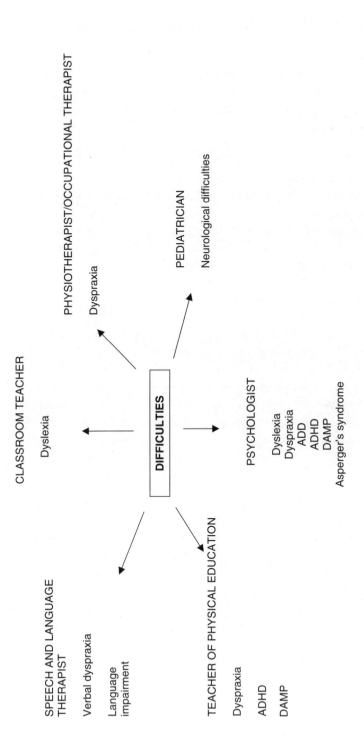

*Figure 1.1* Diagnostic difficulties

in games with other children, or going swimming where she has to get undressed and dressed again – this is a real difficulty for her. Generally she seems to have no confidence in herself at all. Her teacher says she comes into class, sits quietly and just dreams the day away. She has a wonderful imagination and sometimes will tell a long story, but getting her to write even a short one is practically impossible yet she can write and spell. If she isn't hurried, her writing is neat, but she only offers a few words. Sometimes we worry that the imaginative scenarios become too real for she is so immersed in the characters and the plot that she doesn't seem to differentiate between that and reality.

In most curriculum areas she'll begin a task and then she gives up. She says she can't remember what to do next so she drifts into a world of her own and then comes out with a poem that is simply amazing. She doesn't smile when the other children give her a clap for this – they just don't understand her and so no one has her as a friend now. It's agony for her and for us.

She can follow instructions if they are given one at a time but finding her way in a new environment is impossible for her. She loses her coat regularly and never feels the cold so she doesn't miss it. At school she is always being scolded and at home too I'm afraid that we sometimes get impatient because she can't or won't hurry up and has no idea about getting herself organized for the day. She is bright I'm sure, but she's in all the bottom groups and so schoolwork doesn't motivate her either. What's wrong and what can we do?

This real life scenario perhaps helps to explain why discrepancies in assessments sometimes occur. Leah doesn't communicate her feelings to other children readily – could she have Asperger's syndrome? And yet she has a wonderful imagination and can pretend – competencies which some children with Asperger's find difficult. She has the planning and organizing difficulties often found in children with dyslexia, yet she can read and spell. Could she then have dyspraxia? She has difficulty with getting dressed and that involves hands crossing the midline of the body which is difficult for children with dyspraxia and she has the forgetfulness and the lack of awareness of temperature which some dyspraxic children display. She avoids any kind of contact activity, but her fragile build could explain that. She doesn't pay attention – could she have ADD? But she is very still and quiet so that rules out hyperactivity or impulsivity. Certainly assessments like this are complex!

Table 1.1 Some key overlapping difficulties

| | Sensory perception/ integration | Attention concentration | Short-term working memory | Inconsistency in performance | Difficulty following instructions | Planning, organizing, sequencing | Language difficulties | Phonological awarenes | Literacy | Poor concept of time | Movement fluency | Confused laterality | Rhythm and timing | Social communication |
|---|---|---|---|---|---|---|---|---|---|---|---|---|---|---|
| | 1 | 2 | 3 | 4 | 5 | 6 | 7 | 8 | 9 | 10 | 11 | 12 | 13 | 14 |
| Dyspraxia | ✓ | ✓ | ✓ | ✓ | ✓ | ✓ | | | | ✓ | ✓ | ✓ | ✓ | ✓ |
| Dyslexia | ✓ | ✓ | ✓ | ✓ | ✓ | ✓ | ✓ | ✓ | ✓ | | | ✓ | ✓ | ✓ |
| Asperger's syndrome | ✓ | ✓ | | ✓ | ✓ | | ✓ | | ✓ | ✓ | ✓ | | ✓ | ✓ |
| Specific language impairment | | | ✓ | | ✓ | ✓ | ✓ | ✓ | ✓ | | | | ✓ | ✓ |
| ADHD | | ✓ | ✓ | ✓ | ✓ | | | | | | | | | ✓ |
| ADD | | ✓ | ✓ | ✓ | ✓ | | | | | | | | | ✓ |
| DAMP | ✓ | ✓ | ✓ | ✓ | ✓ | ✓ | | | | ✓ | ✓ | ✓ | ✓ | ✓ |

## The overlap of indicators

At first glance it would seem straightforward that all children presenting with certain difficulties would be given one diagnosis or 'label'. However, each syndrome or specific learning difficulty has a number of indicators and while there may be a key difficulty which would seem to point to one particular condition, there can also be a significant overlap or co-occurrence of others and this confuses the picture. (This has happened with Leah (Case study 1).) As many as 50 per cent of children diagnosed as dyslexic may well have the poor coordination which is also seen in dyspraxia. Poor concentration or poor short term memory (a possible component of both dyslexia and dyspraxia) may also be found in children with attention disorders or communication difficulties yet they may have been diagnosed as having Asperger's syndrome. Other children with dyslexia may be nimble and dexterous while children with dyspraxia may have no reading difficulties at all, yet both may find difficulty making friends – a symptom which can also present in children with Asperger's syndrome and SLI. Diagnosis can never be easy when children present different blends of difficulties at different levels of severity and when symptoms overlap between conditions (see Table 1.1). Kirby (1999) explains, 'it is very difficult to find the "pure" child'. Recognition of this results in some children having a double label, e.g. dyslexia and dyspraxia and even then traces of other conditions may be present too. These difficulties will be dicussed in Chapters 3, 4 and 5.

Some important indicators, e.g. low self-esteem, can result from the difficulties which the children experience. Many children with specific learning difficulties have low self-esteem arising from frustration and disaffection.

## Variability of performance

A further problem for those making the assessments is that children may be able to do a task satisfactorily one day yet be totally unable to comply the next. For children with specific learning difficulties, progress is often erratic and this makes both diagnosis and prognosis very tricky. Added to that is the frustration this brings to both teacher and pupils when earlier teaching and successful efforts seem to have been in vain. Recognizing this fluctuation also explains why detailed observational records of the children must accompany them if any 'outsiders', i.e. people who do not know the children well and have not had the opportunity to watch them interacting in various learning environments, are involved in making assessments. It also shows why parents and staff who have built sound relationships with the children and who know their 'performance' on tasks over time should always be consulted, for often the child at school and the child at home appear as very different beings.

Case study 2

Scott, aged nine, has dyspraxia – his most severe difficulties are in planning movements, especially when they have to be done quickly, and in following a sequence of instructions. This means that he has great difficulty in games such as football where kicking the ball with some accuracy and following the rules of the game are important skills. Despite his 'having two left feet' (to quote Scott's self-evaluation), and his tendency to score an own goal, 'because I can't remember to go the other way when we change ends', Scott was rarely left on the sideline. Laughing and smiling at his own mistakes, he came over as a carefree youngster who could cope when the other children jeered 'not again, Scott – it's the other way'. His teacher explained that he was lucky to have the resilient personality which would help him through. She was aware that other children with Scott's difficulties were more vulnerable and 'needed lots more support'. However, Scott's parents had another tale to tell, for when Scott came out of school he 'exploded' with all the frustrations of the day. His behaviour at home was rapidly deteriorating and his parents were worried that they could no longer communicate with their son in a helpful way. 'Scoring an own goal' was no longer something to be shrugged off – it was a cause of lasting shame, anger and frustration. Scott's parents despaired of being able to keep his self-esteem high. His difficulties were public, open to the scrutiny of his peer group, and although Scott was a fluent reader and was often praised in class, he valued this skill much less than being able to play games well. Only his parents could provide insights like this when the assessment was made.

How then is the most pertinent information to be collated? The class teacher has a vital role in building a profile and these first-line assessments may indicate the need for a more formal 'external' assessment later. Unfortunately parents and teachers who know their children well, often feel frustrated when 'after all the trouble setting up the tests' and 'contacting psychologists to carry them out, the results show us nothing we didn't know already'. They become angry that the children have had the stress of taking a test in unfamiliar surroundings with people they didn't know. Why then is a formal test of this nature carried out? A standardized test provides measurable descriptors which identify the depth and range of the children's difficulties. Arguably these results are less subjective and therefore less likely to be seen as biased (by being conducted by people who know the children well). Additionally, policy makers may insist that there must be a cut-off point differentiating between those that have and do not have any condition. Objective measurements compared to the age-related norms of behaviour can be used to make this distinction. Furthermore, testers are aware of the bias produced by stress. They do their best to reduce it perhaps by chatting with the children in a friendly fashion beforehand to build some sort of relationship, by making the test items fun and by starting with the easier items so that the children experience success. When the test items find the children can no longer succeed, there is never any sense of blame or failure communicated to the children and if the test is repeated at intervals, there is a positive, objective record of the children's progress. This spells out exactly what the children can now do for a limited number of skills and competencies.

It is this limitation which must be carefully considered so that the results are not applied generally to include some competence which was not tested. If, for example, planning and organizing is a key difficulty, the children must have several opportunities to show their competence in this area. The test items must be critically scrutinized in this way to ensure that they are comprehensive enough to do their job, i.e. that they 'measure' the right things. They must also be appropriate for children who have difficulties. Furthermore, if the tests are to be repeated over the duration of a programme, the items must also be able to show small areas of progress or regression over time.

Results from standardized tests can usefully sit beside the less formal assessments which will give a more general picture of the children's daily coping skills and cover critical areas such as the ability to form relationships and the development of empathy, i.e. their social skills. In these kinds of assessments, actions speak much louder than words. This is because the 'right' or 'approved' answer (e.g. how they would act if one of the children they really didn't care for was hurt) may well be worked out by the children although their observed behaviour would not bear this out.

## What sorts of things should be assessed?

Some aspects of behaviour, e.g. the skill to catch a ball or balance on a bench or identify letter blends or interact with friends, can be identified quite readily. There are many others, however, which are harder to spot, e.g. how the children approach new learning situations or the various ways in which they prefer to learn different skills. These traits provide vitally important information yet not every assessor has eyes that can see or even the time to make enough detailed observations to compile a comprehensive profile.

Observers need to understand rather than make spot judgments. If, as just one example, some children are always last to be chosen for a game and become very tense with the misery of it all, is it any wonder that they can't throw the ball in the right direction or remember the rules of the game when they do get to play? Despair, tension and frustration can so easily affect competence. Personality traits must also be considered. Whether children are resilient and can bounce back after something going wrong or are sensitive and vulnerable, tending to despair, is a very important observation which can't be readily 'measured' by testing, yet many incidents and responses can be encapsulated in a daily diary. And so assessors who do not know the children very well, have to look beyond their immediate performance to understand the complex thought processes and self-evaluations which may cause the children to behave as they do.

To make a full assessment which will lead to the most helpful intervention or support strategies being planned – and this is surely the whole point of doing it – observations need to be made in each aspect of the children's development: intellectual, social, emotional and perceptual–motor. In addition, it is important to remember that all these aspects interact to make the children what they are, and that progress or regression in one aspect affects all of the others (see Figure 1.2).

### What kind of things come under each heading?

Of course these 'things' don't happen in convenient boxes as shown in Table 1.2; nonetheless it does show the range of competencies which have to be acquired in different areas of development. This division is artificial because of the knock-on effect any change has, right across the board.

## Other influences on assessment

Think of the children coming to nursery who, despite being very competent at home, regress to an earlier developmental stage, wetting pants or sucking thumbs or speaking in a high-pitched voice, because they have been overwhelmed by the new learning environment or the sea of unfamiliar faces. Such responses mean that their physical development has been temporarily affected by the new intellectual and/or social and/or emotional demands, but it would be crass to make one isolated assessment and tick a box indicating concern.

Sometimes even older children fail to learn as they should because they have fallen out with their friends or feel their world has collapsed because they don't

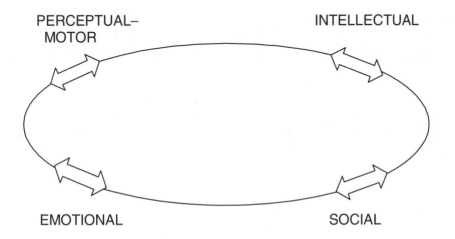

Figure 1.2 The interacting aspects of development

Table 1.2 Lists of competencies

| Social development helps children | Perceptual-motor development helps children | Intellectual development helps children | Emotional development helps children |
| --- | --- | --- | --- |
| build relationships with others | control their movements with increasing dexterity | develop knowledge and understanding of the world | approach new situations with confidence |
| learn from others | move effectively and safely in different environments | develop language and communication skills | express feelings and emotions |
| interact appropriately with adults and children | develop spatial and kinesthetic awareness | develop the capacity to think logically and rationally | pretend to be someone else |
| cooperate in group situations | develop the abilities that underlie skilled performance | make informed decisions | cope with anxieties and be more resilient |
| take the lead role in decision making | know how to organize sequences of movement | develop mathematical and scientific concepts | enjoy open-ended problems |
| take the subsidiary role at times | become involved in health giving activities | solve problems | appreciate works of art/music/dance |
| learn to empathize, i.e. understand different perspectives | enjoy participating in sports, gymnastics and dance | think creatively about new ways of doing things | become aware that others have needs too |
| understand how events affect others | be confident in tackling new movement challenges. | concentrate on the task at hand | cry if they want to |
| develop socially acceptable behaviour in different circumstances | | cope with specialized learning in the classroom and at home. | understand the perception of other people |
| make decisions (social and/or moral) and stay with them | | | develop altruism |
| appreciate the value of friendship | | | appreciate the atmosphere in e.g. a church |
| develop altruism, i.e. caring for others at some cost to oneself. | | | be innovative and imaginative. |

have the 'right' kind of schoolbag or trainers or computer game. In this case their perception of the social environment is negatively influencing their intellectual competence. Once these temporary blips are overcome, the children's learning can get back on track, so accurate assessment can't really be done in a context-free void. It needs lots of reflecting and asking, 'why?'

The debilitating effect of any illness or allergy must be considered in any assessment plan for lethargy due to medication can come over as reluctance to cooperate and skew any non-verbal assessment.

Important too is the 'equipment' the children have when assessments are made. Shoes or trainers with inflexible soles can prevent the rocking action which should happen in walking and give the child an awkward clumping gait. Children who find catching difficult can often manage if a softer ball removes the fear of being hurt while a triangular pencil grip and a steady inclined board on their desk can make a big difference to children whose writing is poor.

There is also the important question of whether the children are motivated to try at all! Boredom can easily be mistaken for non-compliance or even inability to cope.

All these are important details which could be overlooked, yet they are significant enough to skew any assessment score.

Assessing children in this way, i.e. across all aspects of development, gives a comprehensive picture and ensures that no aspect is overlooked. Furthermore, identifying the children's ways of coping across the four domains (see Figure 1.2) lets assessors see whether the children have found ways to disguise their difficulty. Some children may claim that they 'prefer' to take a book and sit alone at break times but truth be told, this is because they fear the rejection or the blank looks when they try to make friends and somehow land up alienating those they approach. Their 'coping strategy' or chosen way of covering up their difficulty is not really constructive at all, beyond making the situation tolerable and yet a passing adult might observe the children as being 'happily' engrossed in a book.

Making observations and assessments needs prior understanding of the children and much contextual information, e.g. how often they act in this way, if and how they change according to circumstances and, most importantly, is the children's way the most helpful that can be tried? Observant adults who are with the children for extended periods of time are surely the best judges of whether support is required and what form it should take.

## The timing of formal assessments

The timing of any assessment is another thorny issue. Questions about the possible effects of maturation are often asked, e.g. 'At what point might children with poor expressive language be considered to have a specific language impairment rather than an immaturity?' or 'Will increasing strength and longer limbs not reduce any movement difficulties the children have?' or 'Will experience not overcome their difficulties?' These are all important questions, yet it is difficult to provide answers which can apply to each child. These depend on the degree of difficulty the children show, what exactly these difficulties are and the commitment to regular practice which can be expected. Generally speaking, however, specific help is essential and the earlier it can be given the better. Then difficulties can be minimized before they do lasting harm. The assessment and diagnosis may have produced a label – and there are pros and cons to administering it (see Chapter 2) – but at all times reassurance can be given that 'the label need not stick' (Caan, 1998) and that many symptoms respond favourably to recognized treatments (Munden and Arcelus 1999).

## Regular practice

Children never fail to surprise by what they can achieve and regular daily practice/ overlearning can make a huge difference to the children's level of skill (Macintyre 2002). A claim like this, however, must be treated with caution.

Practice times should come when the children and their parents are fresh. Imposing sessions of 'exercises' when the children are tired and the adults are fraught, can only be counterproductive. It is not difficult to understand why children who find concentrating difficult and have to struggle to stay on task all day long, can be reluctant to start any extra practice at home. If they suspect that more frustration and failure follows they are sure to find strategies to avoid it happening.

Sustaining a positive atmosphere at practice time is incredibly important. Somehow the activities must be enjoyable and seen as being 'cool' – for after all these are extra things which other children do not do. The children must also be able to recognize that they are making progress. When this is slow or erratic the children can easily become dispirited.

### Too much practice

All those concerned to provide extra support for the children have to consider the overall demands that are being made. If, for example, the children are in a 'spelling group' in class – often the bottom group – and they find they have extra spelling with a support for learning teacher, is it any wonder that spelling practice at home quickly loses any appeal? Adults who try too hard may only succeed in turning the children off. Moderation has to be the name of the game.

## The importance of routine

Many children, especially those with dyspraxia or those with Asperger's syndrome, are more comfortable and confident staying within a tightly structured routine. Even small deviations such as an outing or a television programme happening five minutes later than planned may cause real distress. Furthermore, 'treats', if these involve breaks in routine, can give more stress than pleasure. Perhaps short-term memory difficulties contribute both to this and to planning and organizing problems. Recognizing that anticipated events will still happen despite the delay and rationalizing the adjustments which need to be made are competencies that are beyond many children's ability to cope.

It is likely that the children internalize a known routine to give them security and so overreact (or so it seems to people without this problem) when schedules have to be changed. Calm explanations before and *after* the event (showing the children how well they managed to adjust) are necessary in the hope that transfer of learning will occur to build confidence for changes which happen in the future.

## Complex terminology

Surely simplifying terminology or at least having a clear understanding of terms is the way to foster easy interaction and trust amongst the adults striving to help a child and yet parents and different groups of professionals can feel confused, horrified or belittled by not understanding some of the descriptors. Parents, already likely to be concerned and alarmed, may not wish to make their 'inadequacies' known to professionals; they may not explain that they do not understand the terminology and so misunderstandings and often unnecessary worries arise. This even happens between different groups of professionals.

One very distressed parent explained,

> I nearly fainted when they said, 'we suspect co-morbidity', I honestly thought they were telling me that Jason had a terminal illness and I didn't hear another word they said. I knew he had dyslexia and I could cope with that because I've never been much of a speller myself, but co-morbidity? What's that?

What indeed? In medical parlance the word, used properly, means that one patient has two conditions, e.g. diabetes and arthritis. They need not be connected in any way. However, in education the term has come to mean the overlap which occurs within different specific difficulties. Co-morbidity is therefore a misnomer, co-occurrence being a more precise term. And so when children have more than one condition, e.g. dyslexia and dyspraxia, they can be said to have co-occurring dyslexia and dyspraxia. Not all indicators of each difficulty are necessarily shared, but when they are, they are referred to as 'commonalities'. When this occurs, programmes of activities to help the one child should be effective in helping the other.

Kaplan and her colleagues have also been perplexed by the possible misuse of terminology. To overcome this, they suggest the term ABD (atypical brain development) is used, because 'that can be used to address the full range of developmental problems that are found to be overlapping much of the time in any sample of children'. They explain further, 'all these children, for various reasons, have skills that place them at the low end of at least one ability continuum'. The term ABD, they explain, is not in itself a disorder, but 'an integrative concept – the expression of which leads to varying symptoms across individuals' (Kaplan *et al.* 2001).

Parents and professionals, perhaps even one step removed from being involved in teaching the children but nonetheless interested and wanting to understand, are anxious to know the source, the implications, the duration, the severity and the prognosis of any difficulty. This must be explained in language that everyone can understand. If not, confusion, misunderstandings and anxiety will surely follow – states which could encourage people to try expensive, quick-fix 'cures' which may not have been thoroughly researched and give unrealistic expectations of success. Many parents are desperate to try anything that 'someone' says works. They have to be helped to understand the most reliable ways and so be encouraged to be knowledgeable partners in the programmes developed to support their children.

## Helping children together

The fact that there are so many children with overlapping difficulties does mean that groups of similar-age children can enjoy programmes of activities together. This helps the children's social skills as they learn to cooperate, to take turns, to wait patiently for other children and to appreciate the difficulties other children have. It also enlarges the scope of what can be done, e.g. several joining in a mini game of passing a beanbag (more ideas in Chapter 5), and above all it means that the activities can be suitable for all the children in that particular age group.

The following chapters will revisit the key issues in more detail and alongside the explanations of the children's difficulties are strategies to help. The aim is to build on the strengths the children have and so to keep their self-esteem high.

There are many texts on each specific condition. As this book concentrates on the overlap of difficulties, only brief descriptions of each condition are given alongside some recognized lists of criteria for diagnosing each difficulty. These are in the Appendix.

# Chapter 2

# Assessment

## Communication, investigation and speculation

The aim of this chapter is to show how schools can initiate or extend good practice by recognizing how the assessment process can be facilitated by communication, investigation and speculation. Parents, teachers and others can be encouraged to share information, to monitor progress and to build a profile which will explain their children's difficulties and pinpoint positive ways to help.

## Communication

### First with parents/carers

Often the best place to begin the assessment process is by talking with parents. Clear communication is essential amongst all those who interact with children, for each will be able to contribute observations and assessments from different facets of the children's lives, thus empowering the professionals in school to offer appropriate support. Information, built from descriptions of the way children tackle everyday activities at home, can complement 'how they get on in school' observations to provide a richer picture than any standardized test.

An ideal place to begin is the teacher/parent interview which happens when the children are enrolled for nursery. This allows parents to ask questions and share any concerns with the staff. 'Time to share' is important because then an open channel for communication can be set up and parents and teachers can become 'real' partners in their children's education. So often at such meetings, administration, i.e. sharing rules and procedures, takes over from any quality interaction which would allow discussions about the child and a shared trust to be established. Planning times when staff can be free allows important issues such as confidentiality and security of gathering and storing information to be on the agenda.

Case study 3

Ann, a new support for learning teacher in an inner-city school, suspected that one of the children in her class had a reading difficulty. Appreciating the possible genetic impact in dyslexia, she consulted her head teacher to find out if she could ask the child's parents whether any other member of the family had reading difficulties. To her surprise she was informed that that would be an invasion of privacy and that no such questions could be asked.

Yet the sharing of such information, e.g. a family history of any kind of difficulty, can help teachers to be proactive in their assessment and support of their children. This would seem to be beneficial, so why does it not routinely occur? Some parents may doubt the result of any earlier assessment and hope, given their perception of progress, that the staff's assessment of their child in a new environment will be different. Some may fear being thought pushy or over-anxious if they seek more of the staff's time to share observations while some may even doubt if their 'hunches' would be relevant. For other parents, just getting into school can be fraught with feelings of inadequacy or even self-blame if they consider that their parenting skills may have been lacking in any way. They may even consider that they are to blame for any difficulty their child has. All of these factors act against open and frank communication. When that doesn't happen, however, parents have to recognize the possible knock-on effects, e.g. that if the confirmation of a difficulty is delayed, the school's request for extra support, perhaps in the form of another nursery nurse or classroom assistant, may be too late for that particular session.

Another possibility is that parents may genuinely not recognize the 'signs and symptoms' of difficulties in their children at all, especially if this is a first child with no siblings for comparison. One important example concerns crawling. Some parents, quite understandably, think that because their children missed a step, moving from sitting to walking without any intermediate stage, they were doing well. Imagine their upset when they later realize that some children don't crawl because they can't crawl – i.e. they have not mastered the complicated coordination and patterning which would allow it to happen. Indeed, the inability to crawl may just possibly be one of the early signs of learning difficulties (Portwood 2000; Macintyre 2001). This is why re-teaching crawling is part of many early intervention programmes.

Another area of concern which may be missed is the children's speech and language. At home the parents' ears will be 'tuned in' and as they also interpret meaning from the child's body language, they may not realize that their child cannot be understood by anyone else. Yet early speech and language support is highly desirable, even essential for these children. Or they may consider baby talk charming long beyond the time when it should be overtaken by a more adult way, not realizing that poor articulation or limited vocabulary is a real impediment to learning and socializing at school. Alternatively, if the parents have concerns yet don't share them, then the teachers may be misled into thinking that the child is quiet because of the new environment rather than suspecting a speech and language difficulty. After all, many children with speech problems can understand all that is going on and respond appropriately. In a class of thirty-three children, their difficulties could be missed until a more formal assessment occurs.

Case study 4

*Kieran explained*

> When I'm asked a question in class, my tummy just goes all tight and I feel sick and I know that although I know the answer I won't be able to get it out in time. I am frightened my voice will go all shaky and somehow the words get all jumbled up – at least that's what Mum says. She tells me to take my time and concentrate on what I've got to say but it would be much better if nobody asked me anything. I sit and look at my book but the teacher often says, 'Wake up Kieran and tell us what you think', and that's what I hate.

Someone in school has got to recognize dysarthria or cluttering, i.e. aspects of speech which prevent others from understanding what is being communicated, and contact the speech and language therapists for help.

## Communication with the children

Sometimes, especially with older children, the best way to find what difficulties they have can be to ask them. They are often able to explain what their most pressing difficulties are and this provides pointers for the most appropriate support. If they are not able to do this – if they are unsure what things are the most difficult or become distressed through trying to explain – teachers can then try to establish the point of breakdown. This can be done by reflecting on the learning process, considering the ways any material was presented and suggesting an alternative mode. The strategies implicit in good teaching are the same for all the children whether they have specific learning difficulties or not. There is no other magic formula – just good teaching which involves having a range of strategies to match each child's needs.

The children also need to be reassured that they have strengths and abilities in many areas and that they can use these to help them overcome their difficulties. An example would be asking children to give a pictorial response, e.g. a drawing, a diagram or a flow chart rather than a verbal or written response. Recording stories on a tape recorder is another strategy which enables the children to speak at a pace that is comfortable for them, thus avoiding the writing and/or speaking difficulty which was denying them success.

The most important point to communicate to the children is that they are not to blame for any difficulty they have. If they cannot progress as others do they quickly feel inadequate. Moreover, if their parents have been unable to access early help everyone feels let down by the system. 'Getting help' may not be straightforward, yet there must be access to support or reflections like Jack's will continue to happen.

---

Case study 5

*Jack, aged 12*

> All my life I've felt inadequate. I knew I couldn't do things other people did without thinking but no one explained why. I got teased at school – 'Butterfingers' wasn't so bad but when someone called me 'Jammy Dodger' it stuck and all the kids in the playground thought that was hilarious. That came about after I had to miss PE and do extra maths to catch up. I was pleased to get out of all that running around because that's something I'm not good at, but as usual something happened to spoil it. I'm good on the computer and can help some of the others in the class with that, but making things is just impossible. The teachers try to help, but sometimes this makes things worse because the others think I'm getting extra attention and call me 'teacher's pet'. Or they ask me, 'What's wrong with you?' and I can't say 'everything', and anyway, how can they sort everything? There's no point answering at all.

---

### Communication with colleagues

A class teacher suspecting a movement difficulty in children would clearly consult a teacher of physical education if there was one in school. Such collaboration might result in the PE teacher carrying out a further assessment of the children's movement patterns (gross, fine and manipulative skills), which might lead on to a standardized assessment by a physiotherapist or psychologist. Alternatively, if the difficulties were less severe or if specialist input was not available, the children could be involved in a perceptual–motor programme (see Chapter 5 for ideas). Very often in these situations, the PE teacher would plan the content of the programme, oversee the first sessions and then assist in carrying out assessments at intervals, leaving the day-to-day running in the hands of classroom teachers, assistants and nursery nurses. Obviously this is most effective when all the personnel can share their observations, their ideas for developments and their delight when the children's performance improves.

Playground supervisors and other non-teaching personnel can become involved too, answering such questions as, 'Have these children friends in the playground?' or 'Do they join in running games?' or 'Are they alone most of the time?' – or even 'Are they being bullied?' Other pertinent observations can come from questions such as, 'Can they use a knife and fork in the lunch hall?' or 'Do they have difficulty cutting their food or opening their beakers of juice?' or 'Are they too tired to be able to do any of these things well?' All of these kinds of questions are so important because they reveal how the children cope outside the classroom, i.e. when they are involved in the activities of daily living.

### Communication with other professionals outside school

Adults at home and teachers at school can be reassured that there are other professionals to confirm or refute their assessments and to suggest programmes for support. To ensure the best outcome, health and education have to talk. Difficulties are sure to arise if the child goes off somewhere to have an assessment and the report is delayed or only describes what the child can do and does not contain advice for the classroom or the home. However, psychologists, physiotherapists and occupational therapists have their own set of problems too. If they do not know the child's home context they can't be sure that their advice will be followed through. They are familiar with complex terminology specific to their own field and may not have time to explain to teachers, parents or children exactly what this means. They can be discouraged and perplexed by having too large a caseload and not feeling they are giving enough individual help. The question of how these issues can be resolved is not easy to answer when the number of children with specific learning difficulties is increasing. Hopefully, new collaborations (which are the foundation stones of the New Community Schools in Scotland where different sets of professionals are on the same campus) may go some way to resolving this problem.

The new policies on inclusion, written to ensure that every child is given the support which would enable them to be on an even playing field as they learn, are admirable. The hope is that management and support staff are given time and resources to allow them to make full use of their expertise.

## Investigation

The usual method of investigation is through assessment – both ongoing informal assessment which allows the teacher to plan strategies for support, and formal assessment which is most often used for profiling or reporting home. Each has advantages and disadvantages. Assessment is needed to pinpoint a child's level of performance; explain lack of progress; identify strengths and difficulties; and reveal preferred learning styles. It can also be used to rank children and in so doing cause some children stress and anxiety. Assessing children is a complex process and should be undertaken with care, with a specific purpose in mind and with the effect on the children as the first consideration. Any assessment should be used to inform future teaching plans.

Assessment therefore takes many forms. Formal, standardized assessment provides a 'score' which, when compared to a 'norm', gives an indication of how children perform in relation to their peers. This can be useful, but in the case of a reading test administered to a child experiencing difficulty in this area, may do no more than inform the teacher that the child is reading two or three years below their age. Usually this is not a surprise. The test has confirmed what was suspected. National tests, standardized reading tests and movement tests, e.g. the ABC test of motor impairment, are examples of such tests. If they are given regularly, they can also monitor progress over a given period.

It must be remembered, however, that formal, standardized assessment only gives a picture of a child on one particular day and that there are many reasons why that child may have under-performed. The child may be unwell, may have been unsure of what was being asked, or may not have related positively to the tester if an external agency was involved. To overcome this, testing should take place in a familiar setting and be conducted by someone who is familiar to the children. It is also very important that summative assessments which produce 'a result' are supplemented by formative or diagnostic ones which concentrate on the process of learning. These show how the children have developed the knowledge, skills and understandings that they have acquired. If a reading test is used in a diagnostic way, the *kinds* of errors the children made in the process of taking the test can be revealed. A reading assessment such as a miscue analysis, where the teacher identifies the exact nature of the children's mistakes as the activity progresses, can highlight specific areas where further support or overlearning may be required.

Much assessment is curriculum-based and the class teacher may want to give a short test to ensure learning has taken place. A spelling test given after a particular pattern or group of words has been covered is one example of a quick and easy way of discovering whether learning has occurred. The disadvantage is that words tested shortly after a piece of teaching only confirms that the words are held in the short-term memory. Opportunities for overlearning must constantly be given to ensure that they transfer into the long-term memory and so provide a resource for future use.

## Behavioural and dynamic assessment

Some forms of assessment, e.g. behavioural and dynamic assessment, are particularly suited to children who have specific learning difficulties. The first, behavioural assessment, based on observation and note-taking, can reveal much about the learning strategies the children use. It can show how children tackle a learning task, e.g. whether they are confident or reluctant and if they understand what to do. This form of assessment is not intrusive but can illuminate the strategies the children choose and pinpoint less successful ones; it can differentiate between misunderstandings and poor attention spans and, in pinpointing the best kind of support, can be vital when considering targets for inclusion in individualized educational plans (IEPs).

On the other hand, dynamic assessment is interactive. It requires the child to be an active partner in the assessment process. The children can explain 'how they got their answer' and in so doing reveal exact points of breakdown. Teachers and children together can then produce an action plan.

When does assessment happen and what is its purpose?

### Pre-school observations.

Different authorities are currently preparing/altering/extending their nursery profiles and transition documents so that a wealth of information about each child passes on to the next stage. This would seem to be very good news, but in fact many teachers question the relevance of so much continuous recorded assessment given the changes that happen between ages three and five or those which occur for the older children in the course of a year. They suggest that if no difficulties are evident then 'it is more relevant to concentrate assessments as near transition time as possible, else we [i.e. the nursery staff] spend all our time assessing, not teaching'. So any format for assessment has to be realistic in its scope and meaningful for those who will use its contents (Macintyre and McVitty 2003). There is also the question of how much attention is paid at the next stage. Perhaps this is due to the gap caused by the holidays. On the other hand, many infant teachers like to make their own judgments rather than be biased by those that are passed on.

If children have difficulties, however, then 'the more information that comes forward the better. This is because the changes in the children's developing competence need to be shared' (Early years' teacher). Another 'snag' in the current system is that the emphasis on being positive means that many nurseries pass on information about what the children can do and do not highlight difficulties. Given the rate of maturation at this very early age, staff are often unwilling to attribute lack of achievement to a specific learning difficulty, preferring to cite 'developmental "delay" which, with maturation, may be overtaken'. They may also be unsure about any 'cut-off point' which would determine whether a long lasting difficulty was present or not. However, these early years are critical building blocks for the future and if as Trevarthen (1997) claims, '50 per cent of all learning happens in the first five years', then it is better to err on the safe side, identify and monitor possible difficulties and offer support.

## Baseline assessment in the first year at school

Baseline assessment, now mandatory in the UK, is the obvious place to begin to investigate the possible presence of a specific learning difficulty. It is important that this is also perceived as a diagnostic tool which can pinpoint actions to be taken in school. The content of each baseline test can vary from authority to authority, but the following areas from the language aspect of learning would be sure to be included.

### Concepts of print

Difficulties here may suggest a lack of pre-school exposure to print so that the children do not make the connection between the symbols on the page and the story that is heard. Reasons are numerous – perhaps a parent is not at ease with the written word, perhaps the household just prefers television to story time, perhaps there is not a library near at hand or money for books may be scarce. For whatever reason, books have not been part of the learning environment. However, a poor concept of print should be noted.

### Letter knowledge

Difficulties here may again simply reflect a lack of exposure, but continued poor recognition may suggest a poor visual memory so constant checks have to be made.

### Phonological awareness

Difficulties here may indicate that children cannot differentiate between the different sounds either singly or when blends are used. They may have an auditory problem or need much practice in linking the sound to the symbol.

### Writing process

Difficulties here may indicate that poor muscle tone in the shoulders, arms, wrists and fingers does not allow the pen or paint brush to be controlled. Or the children may not remember what it is they are to write or how the letters are formed, even though they could do all of this on a previous occasion.

### Post baseline

Some education authorities are now expanding baseline assessments or following them up with a more detailed screening test, e.g. the Durham Baseline Assessment, Singleton's Cognitive Profiling System (CoPs) and Fawcett and Nicolson's Dyslexia Early Screening Test (DEST).

During such tests, information such as the following can be gathered:

- letter sounds
- high frequency words
- letter formation
- expressive language
- ability to say polysyllabic words
- fine motor control (drawing)
- gross motor control
- balance
- attention

This provides the early years teacher with critical information about the children's progress and pinpoints possible areas of concern.

## Speculation

With the communication and investigation areas of the assessment process complete, the class teacher is in a position to proceed to the next stage – speculation. In the case of children with specific learning difficulties, scrutiny of the results of both formal and informal assessment will reveal areas of competence and areas of difficulty. Children will have their own particular pattern of difficulties. At this stage it may be premature to confirm the presence of a specific learning difficulty although many experienced teachers will have a pretty good idea of what the outcome could be. The important thing at this early stage is that difficulties have been highlighted and the situation will be monitored. Depending on subsequent progress, this may or may not lead to outside agencies such as educational psychologists being consulted and a specific learning difficulty being confirmed.

As well as speculating about the possible presence of a specific learning difficulty, teachers should also be alert to the possibility of co-occurrence. This means looking beyond any label to assess the whole child.

One of the main problems in the past, however, has been the reluctance of teachers to suggest the possibility of specific difficulties in case their interpretation of the screenings and assessments was wrong. There was also the possibility that the child would 'grow out of it' and so the way forward was 'wait and see'. It is now recognized that this philosophy was misguided and that early intervention is critically important. Furnished with observations, checklists and assessments, it would be appropriate for the class teacher to liaise with learning support staff, the SENCO or the appropriate member of the management team and speculate as to the likely interpretation of the results. Then, even if no other agency is approached, the outcome will be that teaching plans will be drawn up to address the particular needs of the children with support offered in areas where difficulty is noted. The situation can then be monitored and the support evaluated.

### Case study 6

Dale had settled in well to his first year at school and was interested in all that happened in class. He enjoyed the reading programme and read fluently, answering well when questioned. The support materials which accompanied the reading programme took the form of games and computer programmes but Dale appeared reluctant to become involved with these. His teacher wondered why and asked Dale what the problem was. He said that he enjoyed reading but did not like the games and could not, or would not, explain why. Scrutiny of his Baseline assessment, administered in the first term, revealed no particular cause for concern. Classroom observation revealed that he interacted well with the other children. He was 'on task' most of the time in numeracy work and was happy to ask for help if unsure.

Despite Dale's apparent ability to read his teacher watched closely as he read and observed that he looked at the picture rather than the print. When she tried to direct his attention to the print he became confused. On checking the key words out of context it became clear that Dale could not recognize them. She worked out that his aversion to the support materials was due to the fact that he could not, in fact, read the words at all and speculated that he may be dyslexic. An interview with mum revealed Dale always asked her to read each page first and he repeated it after her. Appreciating his difficulty, Dale had quickly devised a strategy which allowed him to 'read' in class. He used his good auditory memory to compensate for his poor visual memory. Appropriate strategies were put in place resulting in Dale being supported from an early age.

## Points of breakdown

The main advantage of assessment is that 'points of breakdown' can be pinpointed (Levine 1994). These can occur at any stage in the learning process. Some examples could be:

- Children bring certain competencies to any learning situation and new learning should build on what they already know. On some occasions, however, teachers, perhaps focussing on the 'average' pupil in the class, make incorrect assumptions about the previous experiences or understandings of those who find learning difficult. A point of breakdown has occurred.
- Children may approach a learning situation with different schemata to that intended by the teacher. As an example consider the word 'pitch'. On hearing this word, most children would be likely to think of a football pitch. A child learning to play an instrument, however, might think of musical pitch. In each of these cases 'pitch' is used as a noun. However, pitch can also be part of an adjective, as in 'pitch-black', therefore some children may visualize darkness. It can also be a verb, e.g. to pitch a tent, and children who have been camping might first visualize this meaning. If the pre-learning is inadequate, i.e. if the children have no understanding of the word at all or if there is confusion because of the context in which it has been used, a breakdown occurs.
- Sometimes the teacher's mode of delivery does not match children's preferred ways of learning. If the main teaching mode is oral, children with auditory processing difficulties will struggle and may well 'switch off'. This is not a deliberate decision not to pay attention but a natural reaction when learning becomes difficult. It is one which adults use too! A different point of breakdown has occurred. Learning could have been eased had the teacher used visual aids or invited the children to participate in a hands-on, practical learning activity.

- Many children with specific learning difficulties process information more slowly than others of the same age. This means that they can be overwhelmed by the teacher's rate of speech. Yet another point of breakdown has occurred.
- Many teachers introducing a new topic give an overview before breaking the learning into smaller steps. Many children benefit from this because they require the 'big picture' as a framework for recall and comparison. If this does not happen these children tend to get lost in the detail of the description. Another point of breakdown has occurred.
- Some children have difficulty processing visual information. They experience distortions in print which required the use of colour to reduce the glare of black on white. If this occurs, a point of breakdown has been reached.
- Many children have short-term/working memory problems. Since their memories cannot sustain a sequence of instructions, they forget what they have to do. Such children are often accused of not listening or paying attention when, in fact, a point of breakdown has occurred.
- The kind of output which is required can cause problems for many children. Clearly a written output is problematic for dyslexic children if spelling is poor or for dyspraxic ones if they have poor control of their pencil, making formulating letters difficult. On the other hand an oral output may be problematic for children with specific language impairments or those who find social communication with their peers difficult.
- Children with specific learning difficulties usually require individualized or differentiated input designed to alleviate their difficulty. If this doesn't happen and they experience continual failure, they will become demotivated. Another point of breakdown has been reached.
- Children with poor attention spans will experience difficulty at the input, processing and output stages of the learning process. Breakdown can happen at any stage.

### Strategies to overcome some common points of breakdown

Lack of progress in any area of the curriculum can indicate that points of breakdown have occurred and the following support strategies can be helpful.

- Ensure that the purpose of the learning is understood by the children and that it is relevant for their background knowledge and their stage of development.
- Provide 'advance' organizers (i.e. pictures or items shown at the start of a lesson to prompt recall). This is essential if children have missed some pre-liminary stages. Sometimes teachers may overlook the paucity of the children's experiences in a particular topic so that the gap between what the children already know and that which they have to learn is too large.

- Provide resources which will reinforce learning through using other modes, e.g. having visual material to back up verbal explanations, or use a multi-sensory approach where children can move to understand the essence of a word (e.g. the smoke swirling can be 'felt' by curling, rising movements of the hands).
- Revisit the topic at the point of breakdown and spend time consolidating the basic facts.
- Find a bypass strategy, e.g. allowing a child to use a calculator or keyboard to reduce stress and provide some sense of achievement.
- Ensure that the basic equipment is the most helpful, e.g.
    o The height of the children's chairs in relation to their desk (feet should be firmly on the floor, not dangling). The chair should be steady, not allowing the children to pivot on the edge.
    o An inclined desktop can help copying from the board (tracking) as there is less need to lift and lower or turn the head. If tracking continues to be difficult then a desktop copy of the work should be provided for the child.
    o A thicker pen or a rubber pencil grip can help hand control and therefore legibility. These come in several shapes to fit different hands.
    o A see-through pencil case can be used to hold timetables and reminders, e.g. 'Hand in lunch money as soon as you get to school today'.
    o The position of the children's desks can make a difference too – they should be near the board if tracking is a problem, and in a quiet spot away from 'traffic' if the children are easily distracted.

### Considering the wider context

But of course children are not just 'there' waiting to be filled up with knowledge and advice which can then be assessed. They are active participants in their own learning and 'things inherited and things learned' and things they themselves wish to do, all impinge on how they learn. Certainly no one can make absolute prognoses about how children will 'turn out' and how they will cope with having a specific learning difficulty. Some children overcome seemingly insurmountable obstacles while others crumble when an outsider would wonder why. These different personality characteristics can influence how children cope and should be included in the assessment process.

Personality differences appear to 'rest on a very basic emotional substrate often referred to as temperament' (Bee 1999), and this affects the way children cope with all kinds of happenings in their lives. What then are some key components of temperament? The list of possible entries, all on continuums, could be large, e.g.

| | | | | | |
|---|---|---|---|---|---|
| sociable | ↔ | reticent; | active | ↔ | passive; |
| emotional | ↔ | calm; | resilient | ↔ | vulnerable; |
| shy | ↔ | outgoing; | extrovert | ↔ | withdrawn; |

| | | | | | |
|---|---|---|---|---|---|
| aggressive | ↔ | gentle; | persistent | ↔ | easily distracted; |
| responsive | ↔ | inhibited; | rational | ↔ | irrational; |
| confident | ↔ | unsure. | | | |

Thomas and Chess (1977) combined these in their descriptors – 'the easy child, the difficult child and the slow to warm up child'.

Temperament also affects how new experiences are welcomed and pursued. Some children love change and actively confront new challenges while others, e.g. children with Asperger's syndrome or some with dyspraxia, are made unhappy by even small changes in routine. If children are predisposed to act in certain ways, these both influence what they choose to do, the spark with which they confront their tasks, and as a result their self-evaluations or feelings about themselves, i.e. their self-concept.

Some of the better known temperamental traits may also be known as cognitive or learning styles because they are the ways in which children naturally tackle learning. Some researchers link certain styles to 'success', although there are arguments both about these claimed links and indeed whether children use the one style to tackle all tasks or whether they can change according to the kind of approach that is required. So, before assigning any style to children, teachers have to observe them tackling different kinds of tasks in different environments. Then they can see if the children consistently act in the same way or if they use different strategies according to the place and the time and the value they put on the outcome. Meadows (1993) would describe this selection of the best way according to the context, 'intelligent behaviour'.

Learning styles can also be seen on a continuum. Two interesting ones which impact on learning and which are of particular interest to children with learning difficulties are

Impulsivity   ↔   Reflectiveness
and
Resilience   ↔   Vulnerability.

The effects of the first one, impulsivity/reflectiveness, can be seen in one task, e.g. reading a text to find the answers to some set questions.

One child, the impulsive one, might skim the text and very quickly announce that the answers weren't there. This could also be seen as an impulsive cognitive or learning style. (Children with ADD, ADHD or DAMP would be likely to act like this.) Generally this approach is not equated with success, and in this instance this was true because the child had not persevered long enough or read the text thoroughly enough to find the answers. This could indeed be a just evaluation, but before ticking any boxes on a checklist, motivational factors would also have to be considered. Was the text at a suitable level of difficulty for the child's reading ability? Was the child interested in that particular text? Were the rewards which were offered, if indeed there were any, in line with things the children wanted to

**MOVEMENT ABILITIES**

Competence in fine, gross and
manipulative skills

Stillness: Control

Rhythm: Timing:
Balance: Coordination

**LEARNING ABILITIES**

Attention: Concentration: Memory:
Motivation: Metacognition

Planning: Organizing: Sequencing

Literacy and mathematical concepts

**PERSONALITY FACTORS**

Resilience/Vulnerability

Reflectiveness/Impulsivity

Self-esteem: Confidence

Motivation: Perseverance

Response to praise

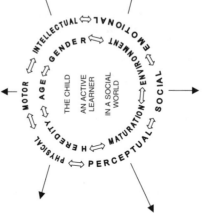

**PHYSICAL AND MOTOR
DEVELOPMENT**

Body Build

Growth and maturation

Reflex inhibition

**SENSORY PERCEPTION and
INTEGRATION**

Vestibular: Visual: Auditory:
Tactile: Kinesthetic:
Proprioceptive: Olfactory
Field independence

**COMMUNICATION**

Initiating: Responding

Relating: Cooperating
Competing
Turn-taking
Making friends

*Figure 2.1* The child: an active learner in a social world

have or would they have preferred to be out at play with some friends and so were resentful at having to do the task at all?

Another child might read the text very slowly and laboriously and come up with the answers that were required. If the child had pondered over issues and considered alternatives before making any decision, that would be seen as a reflective approach and yes, in this instance the outcome has been successful – if waiting time was not an issue. But there are times when it is and then executive functions such as skimming and scanning are the most useful ways of approaching the task. Too much reflection means the child is 'always last', a trait which can irritate others.

Some children are unable to skim and scan (especially those that find tracking difficult) and this causes problems for them when this is the skill that is required. Think of children who need to spot a word within a text. What they need to do is to glance at the lines of text and infer from the shape of the word whether it is there. Children who can't do this, i.e. those who have to read every letter, can't cope with the speed of the task and soon it is too late. Likewise, if the children have to find their own jotter in a pile of others, then quick recognition of the shape of the name on the label is all that is required. Children who have to study every letter or word carefully are left last. Teachers may decide they can't read the words when this is not the case at all – it is the strategy that defeats them. Many children who have dyslexic-type difficulties need this skill to be taught.

Then there are the children who take a long time and don't manage to find the answers at all. Perhaps they weren't sure of what was required or what they were supposed to do. Perhaps they weren't sure how to tackle the task; perhaps they couldn't read the text or understand the meaning; or perhaps, although they appeared to be focussed, they were thinking/dreaming of something much more interesting.

Now to the second example: resilience/vulnerability.

Given the myriad experiences which children must confront as they grow up, most parents hope that their children will have the 'personality to cope' and by that they mean that they will be confident enough to tackle new challenges with enthusiasm and not be overwhelmed by new learning. In the same situation the children's different perspectives can mean that resilient ones focus on the bright side of things and win through, while their more vulnerable peers see the downside and are more easily defeated (Harter 1990; Bee 1999).

The environment in which children grow plays a major part in enabling them to cope. Vulnerable children who have a home where there is lots of encouragement and support can respond to this and become more confident. Resilient children can more easily overcome the problems of a less positive home. It is the combination of vulnerability and disadvantage which children find hard to take. Many children with specific learning difficulties are or become vulnerable because of repeated disillusionment. Even by age four they may feel guilty because they have not succeeded in doing things they would like to do. If their frustration leads to aggression, which the parents punish, the guilt is made worse. Bee (1999) explains that, very often, 'parents of difficult children adapt to their children's negativity by punishing them more often and providing them with less stimulation and support'. And so many have a double handicap – for lots of youngsters, it could be too much to overcome.

All of these issues highlight the importance of understanding the child in the context of the family and the environment before assessment decisions are made.

A final question about temperament which is critically important for children with learning difficulties must concern the children's capacity to select and change. If children are told they are too impulsive, acting without considering the outcome, and that they must be more reflective, take more time, persevere and not give up too quickly; how readily can they change their approach? If teachers explain to the children what they did, then show how another way of coping would have been more successful, how easy is it for the children, not just to change their approach for that task, but to transfer that understanding to other learning experiences? That would seem to be what teaching is all about, but the process, especially for children who cannot use the feedback from one try to help the next or who cannot habituate learning so that transfer from one situation to another can happen, means that any change must be overlearned. If this still doesn't help, it is not difficult to understand the negative effect on the children's self-concept.

## The self-concept

The self-concept is the picture children have of themselves, formed in the process of growing up. It is a tri-dimensional image, 'What I think of myself depends on what I think you think of me'. Cooley (1962) called this process, 'The looking glass self'. This means that as they grow, the children are constantly evaluating the reaction of other people towards them. These reflections – which may be accurate or inaccurate (because of the difficulty of interpreting non-verbal communication) – have an impact in relation to the respect in which the other person in the dyad is held. This process is made even more complex because the 'important people' in the child's environment change. At first the parents are hugely important but then their opinions seem to be supplanted by the teacher in school. Parents will recognize this when their opinions are overruled by what 'Miss so-and-so says'. Later still the peer group take precedence for many children and this time can be especially hurtful for children who lack a stable group of friends.

The self-concept has different components as shown in Figure 2.2.

While the self-concept is the generalized overall picture the children hold of themselves, the self-esteem is the value they put on it. The self-esteem children have depends largely on the distance between their judgment of themselves and the picture they hold of 'what they would like to be', i.e. their ideal self. In the early years of school, physical factors are likely to play a larger part than later when the young people are able to appreciate inner qualities. Hence the youngsters' concentration on the body image component of the self-concept, when 'being fat' or 'looking different' is to be avoided at all costs. Lots of youngsters, for all sorts

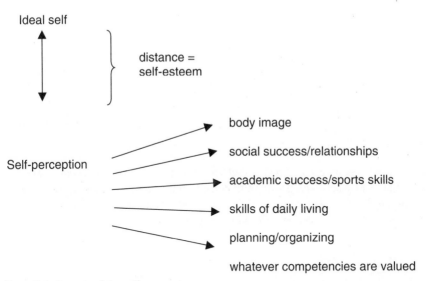

*Figure 2.2* Aspects of the self-concept

of reasons, avoid exercise and eat junk food for comfort or consolation, and this combination may add to their self-evaluation difficulties as it adds to their weight.

The judgments which children make about themselves and in choosing friends, change conceptually as the children grow. External traits, 'I am a girl with lovely fair hair', become less important than more sophisticated judgments, e.g. 'I am a worthwhile person because I go out of my way to help those who are less fortunate than me'. This is due to the development in thinking skills. As the children develop, they make judgments which are not so tied to visual clues. They have the understanding to look below the surface as it were, to see what is there beneath. This cognitive shift influences their actions too – the development of empathy and altruism helping them to be more aware of the difficulties others have and to be sympathetic rather than unaware or uncaring. It is fascinating to realize that as children make these value judgments about other people they are learning to reflect on their own behaviour too and so there is a reciprocal pay-off, children's relationships with others shaping their understanding of themselves. This explains why children with difficulties may find making and keeping friends easier once their peer group have matured enough to 'see' the person underneath.

## Keeping the self-esteem high: giving praise

Through all of those trials and tribulations, the children are coming to know themselves and the part they wish to play in the adult world. The most important thing that adults can do is to boost their self-esteem. Somehow they must convince the children that they have lots of potential to be well-liked 'valuable' people. Keeping young people positive is not easy as many have gleaned quite an accurate picture of their talents and shortcomings, and many children who find an aspect of school life difficult are often over-critical in their self-evaluations, declaring themselves as falling short of some hypothetical norm.

Pope (1988), a head teacher, offers some valuable advice. She explains,

> I have been amazed at how well children accept their difficulties when this is coupled with positive activities to help. Telling a child he is good at something when he knows full well he's not, far from raising his self-esteem only serves to lower it.

And so 'positive realism' without emotional overtones which can make the children feel worse and a differentiated programme of learning activities with achievable objectives seems the best way forward. Repeated failure in front of their peers should never be allowed to happen.

## Giving a label

Closely allied to the considerations about boosting the self-concept is the question of 'giving a label'.

There are pros and cons to 'giving a label' and they have to be considered in the light of the family and the child's temperament and likely reaction to it. The overlap of difficulties making accurate diagnosis problematic and the severity of each child's condition may influence the decision too. What, then, are the benefits of labelling and what are the disadvantages, if disadvantages there be?

### Advantages

- A label offers a description of the difficulty.
- Many parents and children are relieved to have a label – then they know for sure that there is 'something amiss' and that that something can be helped. They can be sure that there is a reason for the child's difficulties which is no one's fault. The children are exonerated from being deliberately awkward or slow to cooperate or unwilling to try.
- The point of giving a label is that the child's right to specific, appropriate help is established. This is likely to be followed by an IEP (individualized education plan) which sets out procedures and strategies (timing, pacing, routines, realistic homework demands in line with other activities children have to do). At school the staff know that a specific learning difficulty has been confirmed and on that basis they can plan their teaching and possibly request extra help. Moreover, if this is the first time they have experienced this particular difficulty, they are likely to read up about it and so be better prepared to help.
- A formal diagnosis means that other accommodations in school can be arranged, e.g. more time for taking tests; having books with fewer words on each page; help with planning and organizing resources.

## Disadvantages

- If the label limits the staff to assisting the difficulties assumed to belong to that disorder, however, it could be of limited use, even do harm. Staff have to look beyond the label to consider other competencies, e.g. how the child copes or fails to cope across all the demands of the day. If the process of labelling meant that the children's difficulties were listed in order of severity, the child would not be made to 'fit' the traditional label but have a profile (crossing several boundaries if necessary) which pointed to the exact kind of help that was required.

    The trouble with this, of course, is that these newer labels would need to be understood and given credibility by all the professionals who used them. Certainly, this move would support Kaplan *et al.*'s hypothesis that the different conditions were manifestations of one cause being demonstrated at different levels of severity – all of which needed to be identified and helped. In this way the help would be specific to the range of difficulties which had been shown.

- Some children are glad to have a label which explains their difficulties and they look forward to group meetings where they can meet children with similar problems, share their experiences and find that they have new friends (to offset taunts that they have none). Other children, however, can be distressed by the suggestion that a label is needed, even if they are told that its purpose is to get extra help. Some youngsters deny that they have difficulties at all.

| Difficulties | Severe | Moderate | Mild |
|---|---|---|---|
| Sensory<br>e.g. listening,<br>body awareness | | | |
| Movement<br>e.g. control in fine skills,<br>control in gross skills | | | |
| Social<br>e.g. communication,<br>making friends | | | |
| Attention/Memory<br>e.g. distractibility,<br>poor recall | | | |
| Language<br>e.g. comprehension,<br>reading, spelling,<br>mathematics | | | |

The above chart could serve as a first record of difficulties – giving a broad picture of areas which need support. It shows the scale of the support which is required and leads to a more detailed analysis in the specific areas.

*Figure 2.3* A first record

They may also resent any suggestion that they should meet other children 'just like them'. Their self-esteem may take a huge knock if the other children are more severely disabled and their own sense of empathy is not well developed. This can be eased if children seen as leaders by their peers are included – hence the plea for carefully chosen groups of children to practise together cooperatively, helping each other and rejoicing in each other's success.

# Chapter 3

# Understanding co-occurrent difficulties

## Sensory perception and integration

Even in the early years, teachers can be pressurized into achieving literacy and mathematical targets. Parents are often anxious, even over-anxious that the skills of reading and numeracy are not delayed. What they fail to realize is that there are fundamental requisites that must be in place before these complex skills can be fully acquired. Perceptual skills fall into this category. If the children are to be confident learners they must be able to take accurate cues from the environment and use these to guide their learning.

## How does this happen?

> All learning takes place in the brain, but it is the body which acts as the vehicle by which knowledge is acquired. Both brain and body work together through the central nervous system, but both are dependent upon the senses for all information about the outer world.
>
> (Goddard 1996)

Throughout life, children are constantly bombarded by information from the environment which comes through their senses and is analyzed in the cerebral cortex of the brain which then transmits instructions to the nerves in the different muscle groups which provide the action. Occasionally just one or two senses are used as key receptors, but more usually a whole group, e.g. vestibular, auditory, tactile, visual, proprioceptive, taste and smell, work together to provide a complex battery of information. Ayres (1972) calls this 'sensory integration' and Bee (1999) 'cross-modal transfer'.

What kinds of guidance does this sensory information provide? Those with intact sensory systems can use sight and hearing and possibly the sense of smell to gauge, for example, the distance of an approaching car or at school where a particular group of friends is meeting. The senses of smell and taste can also advise on the age of food and so indicate what to eat and what to leave well alone. Decisions like these can be made quite simply but more complex actions call on a greater degree of sensory integration.

Think about children learning to ski. Decisions about whether it is safe to ski require a complicated interaction of information from all of the senses working together. The visual sense (sight) shows if there is space on the slope and how steep it is. Sight and hearing (visual and auditory senses) tell how fast others are approaching, while a sense of balance (the vestibular sense) prevents foolhardy decisions if the slope is too steep and keeps the body upright once the run is underway. Nerve endings in the limbs (proprioceptors) relay information about the posture of the body in relation to the skis, while the tactile sense helps the skier grasp the ski pole and feel that the visor is correctly positioned. Finally the kinesthetic sense gives continuous whole body information about where each of the body parts is in relation to the others and in relation to the space around as the skier traverses the slope.

All of these separate pieces of sensory information work together to enable the children to adopt the best position for the run and allow them to adjust it according to the unforeseen demands of the slope on the way down. Of course the skiers need technical skill as well, and the intellectual 'nous' to understand what has to be done, but both of these are dependent on the correct sensory information for success. Unfortunately in some specific learning difficulties this process is less efficient so that the children are not enabled to use information from the environment to aid their learning.

The top part of the simplified figure (Figure 3.1) shows how the perceptual intake from the environment passes to the cerebral cortex of the brain (where it is analyzed and interpreted) and then to the muscle groups which make the response. The arrow from the response or output shows how the feedback from the action is used to inform the next try.

## Efficient learning requires children to have three systems which operate effectively

These are:

1   the afferent system which concerns the reception of sensory information
2   the processing system which organizes/analyzes the information within the brain and
3   the efferent system which concerns the response that is made to the input and the analysis.

Deficit in one or more of these systems can cause difficulty or delay in learning.

The success – or otherwise – of any action provides feedback which will normally be used to guide further responses. Most children who don't manage to jump over a gate are likely to increase the speed of their approach run and use more strength in the take off next time round, even without specific coaching. They use feedback from the first attempt to improve the second try. Unfortunately, not everyone is able to do this. There are three main reasons why.

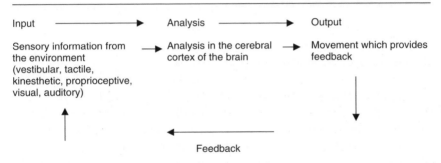

*Figure 3.1* Sensory integration

1    Some youngsters have a motor deficit. This means that while they may recognize that their efforts have been unsuccessful and that their movement response has to be changed in some way, they have not the motor skills to carry this out.

---

**Case study 7**

Alex, aged eight, explained how this difficulty affected him.

My writing is all squiggly and sad [he said in despair, his hands hidden under the table]. I know what I want my hands to do but they just won't do it and so my writing comes out all wrong. I don't want it to be like this but my pencil just won't go the right way! I hold it tightly, I hold it slackly, I try lined paper or stuff with no lines, but it just goes all over the place. In my head I can see it all beautifully, but no matter what I try, it comes out all squint with squiggles that were never meant to be there. Some days it's too black and on other days it's shaky – the computer's much better though. I can get my stories down then. My Mum is saving up for one for me to have at home – I hope she can get it soon.

---

2    Others have a sensory deficit. This means that the information they take from the environment is not 'true' and this can lead to all sorts of misjudgments in spatial orientation (i.e. in placement, distance and direction). The children with these difficulties are often called clumsy because they knock things over or run into walls or fall down stairs and get hurt or hurt others on the way. Their sensory input doesn't give them an accurate picture of where people or things are in the space around them, so mishaps occur all day long.

Case study 8

Listen to Jake, another 8-year-old who exploded,

I'm fed up being called 'clumsy'. It's really very upsetting. I have to use a plastic cup at home because the other ones kept breaking. Mum said not to be in such a rush because I missed the table and the drink fell on the floor but I wasn't hurrying at all. Dad said I wasn't to go near the DVD player without him being there because I would break it. How do you think that made me feel? I know I do knock into things but it's not my fault – boys are just like that, aren't they? The last time Dad got wild with me Mum said, 'Well you are just as bad – you've always had two left feet', and I laughed and laughed and felt much better!

The fact that Jake realized that his clumsiness could be inherited and therefore his difficulties were not his fault offered him some comfort. The cause notwithstanding, however, he has to be helped cope more effectively with all sorts of daily living skills as well as all the practical competencies that are called on in school.

To the casual observer, the ineffective output which both Alex and Jake displayed might appear to be part of the same difficulty, yet the cause is quite different. The first is a motor problem such as that experienced by Alex who did not have the strength in his shoulders, arms and fingers to allow him to control his pencil. The second is a sensory deficit, in Jake's case poor visual-spatial perception which led him to misinterpret the distances between objects and between objects and himself. It is important to distinguish between the two kinds of difficulty so that any intervention can be the most appropriate one. Listening to the children describing their problems is one way of identifying precise difficulties, especially if they are as articulate as these two boys.

3    There may also or alternatively be a planning difficulty when children just don't know what to do or cannot organize resources to make things happen.

When children have sensory difficulties, e.g. in seeing, they may go to an expert in that particular field who may test their 'sight' and find that they can read all the letters on the board, yet not check functional vision, e.g. tracking. This is necessary to ensure that the children can read several lines of close print fluently or copy from the chalkboard without checking and rechecking their place.

Investigations into the other perceptual areas may not be carried out at all. No one may even consider, far less investigate, how the children experience touch (the tactile sense), as just one example, yet understanding hyper (too much), or hypo (too little) sensitivity in any sensory domain is critical in appreciating how the child functions socially and emotionally as well as academically. Hypersensitivity can cause learning delay just as much as hyposensitivity or loss of the perceptual sensation. This can apply to all the senses and as these work together, each one modifying or reinforcing the other, all of them must be understood so that children who have difficulties can receive total, not partial assessment and support.

Each sense will now be considered in turn.

## Vestibular sense

The overarching and most important sense is the vestibular because it controls the ability to keep the body balanced as it moves (dynamic balance) and helps it stay steady when it is still (static balance). It monitors the adjustments which need to be made so that the body can stay poised, even in a changing environment.

The ability to balance is at the very heart of moving and learning. It is the first system to function, even providing orientation and directional cues to the foetus before birth. The vestibular system is located in the inner ear and it controls the adjustments which are needed when the body moves or the environment changes, so keeping the body balanced and controlled. If the system is not intact, the total function of the body is affected. This is because all the different kinds of sensory information pass through the vestibular mechanisms in the brain stem en route to analysis in the cerebral cortex. And so the vestibular sense influences not only balance and movement, but hearing, feeling and seeing as well.

The vestibular system has two main parts consisting of three semi-circular canals and two vestibular sacs – all filled with fluid. Each of these is lined by hair cells which respond to the movement of the fluid by releasing signals along the cranial nerve pathway to the cerebellum. If there is too much fluid sway, motion sickness results. Illnesses such as labyrinthitis (i.e. inflammation of the inner ear) have a similar effect. They cause the sufferers to feel that the floor is coming up to meet them or pitching away and because they are thoroughly disoriented by this, they are sick, fall over and have great difficulty regaining an upright position. Movements become erratic and unsteady and this soon causes a loss of confidence – fortunately this passes once the inflammation has gone.

### Pursuit of vertigo

Amazingly, many young people seek out this sense of confusion, enjoying experiences where they have overstimulated their vestibular system to the point where they are almost out of control. The waltzer at the fair, big dipper rides, skiing and sledging, mountaineering, white water canoeing – all of these activities can give this 'nearly out of control – just at the edge' sensation. Theme parks thrive on the basis of this kind of thrill. The vestibular apparatus must be in good shape to allow such treatment with no lasting effects.

But if the vestibular apparatus is not working properly, and as a result children have a poor sense of balance, they are fighting to overcome gravity so that they may stay in control. All their movement patterns will look unsure and unsteady; often they will tilt and consciously have to adjust to regain the upright position. Walking, especially walking slowly is difficult, while running with any sense of speed and direction can be well nigh impossible. Turning corners sharply is difficult too, so children round them off instead. Even sitting or standing still requires the body to be balanced evenly around its centre. This shows why children with any learning difficulty must have their sense of balance investigated and moves to help it must be put in place.

Those with vestibular difficulties may suffer

- ungainly movement patterns due to a poor sense of balance
- feelings of motion sickness (sea sickness) which distort orientation and sap motivation
- poor organizational skills
- difficulty with directions
- extreme anxiety in activities which involve sudden changes of speed or direction
- slower response times due to orientation/balance problems.

## Auditory sense

The cochlea or auditory apparatus is also in the inner ear, sharing the capsule, the fluid and the nerve pathway with the vestibular system and the two work together to complement or even compensate one another if one is less efficient than it should be. In fact Steinbach (1994) claims that 'sound is not sound' but is the 'manifestation of vibration received into the ear'.

In early childhood, children learn the sounds which signal feeding, bathing, changing and soothing. They also learn the specific sounds of their own language and the meaning inherent in their intonation. The first three years are a critical time for learning language, so parents who are concerned by any lack of response (perhaps noticing a difference when sounds come from behind the child as opposed to reaction when the communication is within the visual field) should request an investigation. Young children need to be involved in conversations, so that they learn, not just the sounds of the words but the 'rules' of social interaction such as turn-taking. Gradually, even through games like peek-a-boo, they learn when it is appropriate to instigate something and when they should 'reply'. Even though this may be in monosyllabic babbling, the smiled approval of the other person in the 'conversation' supports the idea that talking together is a good thing to do. And apart from learning about communication, the children receive satisfaction and support – an enormous boost to their self-esteem.

Children need stories to cultivate their imaginations and to help them learn about sequencing and structure and they also enjoy the closeness and comfort that story time can bring. They are also learning about the rhythm of words and gain lots of enjoyment from the repetition of phrases (think of stories like *The Little*

*Red Hen*). Children who miss this contact and communication, i.e. those who are understimulated, may take some considerable time to catch up. On the other hand a constant bombardment of noise may cause them to 'switch off' so care has to be taken in providing the best auditory environment for each child. Observing the child's reactions to the different 'noises' and noting any time needed to calm or soothe, may be the best way.

There are three kinds of hearing difficulties and all of them hinder learning. They are

- hearing loss,
- poor discrimination between sounds and
- auditory distractibility.

Any hearing loss, either temporary (caused by glue ear or other illnesses, such as colds or ear, nose and throat infections) or a more permanent deafness, always impacts on learning, not only in the academic sense but in social learning needed to make friends and sustain relationships. Children who don't hear well miss the listening and responding opportunities within early interactions and will need support in learning language. Luckily, this is usually available for children who have identified hearing impairments, for early diagnosis and help is essential for the child's development. This is gratifying for parents because they know that steps will be taken with no delay. In this way critical learning periods are not being missed (Trevarthen 1997).

### Auditory discrimination

Children who have difficulties in learning to read and spell can suffer from auditory discrimination problems even though they have acquired speech at the 'correct' time. Some have great difficulty distinguishing between the sounds and this affects their reading and their spelling. If 'p' and 'b' sound the same, or if the children can't distinguish between 'ch' and 'sh' and 'th', then it can easily be seen how these sounds may be used interchangeably in their spelling and writing. Auditory dyslexic children and those with SLI may find it difficult to discriminate short vowel sounds or recognize rhymes and as spelling often depends on a mental rehearsal when the letters are 'heard and seen' phonologically in the head, any confusion means that this 'picture' is likely to be distorted. Repeated practice in a calm environment and learning where in the mouth the sounds are made and how they are produced (input by a speech and language therapist) can give tremendous help.

### Auditory distractibility

The indicators of this are – difficulty in paying attention, difficulty in concentrating for a realistic amount of time, difficulty in holding eye contact and difficulty in being still. Learning in busy classrooms means that there is likely to be some movement and sound beyond the actual teaching that is going on. Most children manage to cut this out of their conscious reckoning and concentrate on the task at hand, but those who have poorly developed listening skills often can't help being distracted by even small sounds or movements. They look up, become intrigued by whatever is going on, get up to investigate further and so lose their place in their work or miss part of the teaching input. On top of this they may be scolded for 'not paying attention' or called 'hyperactive' because they have failed to stay still.

And so, hearing too much, i.e. auditory hypersensitivity, can be almost as disabling as not hearing enough – and in recent years recognition of this has led to attention being paid to 'listening difficulties' as well as hearing ones. 'Listening' is now listed as a separate skill to be assessed as part of any developmental profile, for even in a conducive environment some children require that listening skills are taught … a different premise to assuming that because children aren't hearing impaired, they can listen!

Children's learning can also be affected by which ear is dominant, because there is a difference in the way sounds are transmitted to the language processing centre in the brain. The right ear is the more efficient at processing language sounds, because sounds heard there pass directly to the language centre which is situated in the left hemisphere of the brain. Children who are left-ear dominant have sounds transmitted to the sub-language centre in the right hemisphere and then these have to pass through the corpus callosum to the left hemisphere for decoding. Although the delay is minimal, delay there is, so if the teacher gives a list of instructions, the last may not be accomplished because the delay in understanding the first has hindered the start. Add to this the difficulties experienced by the children with poor short-term memories, i.e. not being able to remember the later instructions in a sequence, and the learning deficit is significant. Yet these are the children who are repeatedly told to hurry up. One wonders how they are to comply.

Lack of ear preference does not solve this problem. It only causes confusion. Why? Because one sound from the right ear may reach the decoding centre ahead of one received by the left ear – yet that may not be the order in which they appear in the phrase. And so to the children, letter, syllable and word reversals appear as logical examples of sounds that have been heard.

In their first three years, children need to fine-tune their hearing so that they can filter out unnecessary distractions and hear their spoken language clearly. They then need to be able to reproduce the sounds they hear and later still, record and reorganize them in written form.

Those with auditory difficulties may experience

- poor or confused reception of sounds
- inability to follow sequential instructions
- confusion of similar sounds
- reduced vocabulary

- poor understanding of the 'rules' of interaction
- reversal of letters, syllables and words
- poor attention span
- poor concentration
- hypersensitivity to sounds resulting in withdrawal or aggression
- poor progress in listening skills.

## Tactile sense

The sense of touch like the vestibular sense, develops early; in fact during the first trimester of pregnancy the foetus will withdraw from any tactile stimulation. This is a defensive response. In the second and third trimester, the sucking and grasping reflexes mature so that at birth being touched offers reassurance and comfort while the developed sucking reflex ensures the babies can be fed and so thrive.

Touch receptors cover the entire body making all of it sensitive to being touched although the most sensitive regions are the lips, the mouth and the hands. This explains why babies investigate the properties of objects through sucking, for the lips and mouth tell about hardness and softness, the temperature and something of the shape and size of the object as well as its taste. Sensitivity in the hands helps discern shape, malleability, weight and size too and it also ensures rapid withdrawal if objects are too hot or sharp.

Within the brain, the area which registers touch, the somatosensory cortex, also deals with pain, temperature, pressure and spatial orientation. Gradually through being touched, information about direction (e.g. sidedness or laterality) develops and this helps general spatial orientation which in turn is necessary for the efficient and effective (balanced) movement which underpins and facilitates learning.

Although the tactile sense has tended to receive less attention than the others, it plays a critical role in development. Indeed, 'touch precedes both hearing and vision as the primary channel of learning' (Goddard 1996) and so its importance should not be underestimated in any intervention to help learning.

The tactile system has been subdivided into 'protective' and 'discriminatory' subsystems (see Figure 3.2). The protective receptors respond to such things as airwaves passing across the body and indicate when it is advisable to go forward or to retreat. They also help the developing sense of body boundary, i.e. where the body ends and the outside world begins. This is essential for deft, precise movement

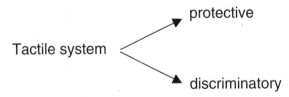

*Figure 3.2* Subdivisions of the tactile system

such as writing or placing objects accurately or judging where the body is in relation to things in the environment, e.g. the edge of the kerb.

On the other hand, the discriminative preceptors take over when the body comes into contact with something or someone. The two sets should not operate together but work singly to do their own job. The protective system operates until the body is touched when the discriminative system takes over.

If this interplay doesn't happen, if the child's protective receptors are too strong then the child will be overly 'tactile defensive' and will withdraw from contact with others. This is the child who rejects cuddles and shrugs off a helpful hand. Often this gives offence through a feeling of being rejected. This can prevent 'communication through touch' happening again and in extreme cases the children can find themselves isolated because no one understands what is wrong. Similarly, the children who won't take hands in a ring or line up close to others or who are overprotective of their personal space may well have this tactile hypersensitivity.

The 'hyper-tactile' child may have a low pain threshold for things like injections which pierce the skin, yet internal pain, e.g. appendicitis, may be tolerated too well leading to delay in getting medical help. Some children actually hurt when their hair or nails are cut and others resist hair washing because of the pain it causes, yet these same children may cope with severe illnesses without complaint. Some children have to have their socks put on inside out because the seams irritate them unbearably (tap dancing socks have no seams which is a tremendous relief for the children and their parents who have one less battle on their hands).

### Case study 9

Lynn, Marie's mother, has lived through experiences like this. She explains,

> We were so relieved when we eventually found a set of clothes which Marie would wear without a crying match and constantly pulling them off no matter where we were. We decided to buy several sets the same because she wouldn't tolerate anything else. I bought larger sizes too and wrote to the manufacturer who sent still larger sizes in different colours. There's no question of Marie going to a school which insists on uniform because she is so unhappy by the least rub of a seam or roughness of the cloth. I think this is why she goes out without her coat when it's freezing. We bought a shower because we thought that that would help her with washing her hair which is always traumatic, but Marie found the jets of water really distressing – her skin is so sensitive, yet she doesn't have a rash. We have been at our wits' end trying to cope!

In summary, there are children who won't be touched, those who touch others too much and those abandoned children confined in orphanages in severely disadvantaged regions who are desperate for tactile communication, yet are deprived of it. To compensate they rock back and forth, back and forth all day long. This is their attempt to gain some sensory stimulation from their very restricted environment. These children want to learn – yet in the past this repetitive action has sometimes been assessed as a sign of intellectual retardation. There are those who are tactile defensive and avoid activities where touch plays a part, e.g. all contact sports, and those who lack the defensive mechanism to protect themselves and so engage in daredevil pursuits because they are not aware of the implicit danger involved.

Those with tactile difficulties may experience

- distress when touched, yet be anxious to touch others
- isolation, having rejected overtures which included touch
- poor awareness of body temperature
- dislike of contact games and sports
- extreme sensitivity to external pain but tolerate internal pain
- a poor sense of directionality (due to not receiving cues from being touched).

## Visual sense

The most obvious benefit of good sight is to see clearly and to be able to distinguish people and objects accurately when they are near at hand or some distance away. It is very helpful in all academic learning if the eyes can cope without strain, for then reading and writing can continue for some time without causing headaches. Efficient vision develops before birth and in the early years. When babies have to be born early, perhaps due to pre-eclampsia in the mother, the doctors try to delay the birth until the twenty-eighth week of pregnancy because that is the time when maturation of the visual apparatus should be such that the child has adequate sight.

'Normal' maturation of the central nervous system should ensure that a complex series of neural connections allows the eyes to function together (convergence) so that a single, sharp image is sent to the brain. The picture seen by each eye must be focussed and the eyes must be able to scan without losing clarity (accommodation). If this doesn't happen, children looking at a letter, e.g. an 'O', can be confused by seeing two overlapping or blurred pictures. These give the wrong information about letter formation and so reading words, interpreting pictures, judging distances, writing on lines – in fact all events in the day – could be hampered by not perceiving the world clearly. Showing a child one letter standing alone and asking for it to be copied (and if this is accurate using two letters side-by-side) is a simple way to check what is being seen.

Children with poor visual discrimination may also have reversal tendencies in both reading and writing, e.g. 'big' may be read as 'dig' (Miles 1991).

## Tracking

Many other kinds of tasks require vision to be used in its functional mode. In copying from the board, in following the path of a ball, in reading lines of text (especially if reference has to be made between two or three passages), the skill of tracking comes into play. This is a skill which defeats many youngsters, yet it is taken for granted by those who do not have such a difficulty. When learning difficulties arise, all kinds of vision have to be tested. This is because reading letters on a chart at the opticians (i.e. testing distance vision) makes a different demand on the visual and perceptual apparatus than does following a moving path or object, i.e. tracking. This ability is also crucial in making spatial decisions, i.e. estimating distance and directions.

Case study 10

Sam, Ian's teacher who was explaining basic mapping skills gives one instance of tracking difficulties. He explained,

When I sat by Ian, a very competent 9-year-old, and said 'Put the sign for the church in the top right hand corner of your paper', he did it with no difficulty. I therefore anticipated that when he had to copy a diagram from the board that would be fine too. But no matter how hard he tried he couldn't transfer what was on the board to the appropriate part of his paper. He realized that when he put the diagram, or at least his version of it, in the centre of his page rather than in the corner, there was no room for the rest of the work, but he couldn't make the shift. After some time looking up at the board then down again to his paper, Ian was able to appreciate that his attempt was 'no use', so we rubbed it out and tried again. I tried to help by asking him to point to where the drawing will go – but that didn't help – once he lifted his finger from that place, he was lost. He literally could not look up then look down and place the diagram accurately. It was all too much!

When children experience tracking difficulties like this, they lose their place and they constantly have to check or readjust their work. All of this takes time and so they fail to keep up with the rest of the class. Their difficulty means that their confidence in the subject suffers, when their intellectual grasp of the material could be highly competent. These children need worksheets alongside or in front of their jotter so that long distance tracking is avoided.

Reading difficulties often stem from poor tracking ability because the eyes fail to move along a line of print smoothly and/or retain a sharp picture. This causes related difficulties because the ability to read accurately and quickly impacts on many curriculum areas and the inability to track objects causes coping difficulties every day. Many motor tasks will cause lots of frustration, e.g. seeing where someone is going, watching races, even following the flight of birds. A tracking difficulty can even lead children into danger. Think of them making decisions about when to cross the road. They must track the oncoming traffic on both sides of the road and make decisions about when they have time to cross. The wrong ones could be disastrous.

NB An inclined writing board can reduce the necessary eye and head movements and in giving some stability, help tracking skills.

### Field independence/dependence

Some youngsters are more field dependent than others. This means that they have difficulty seeing things which project and estimating how far they do, rather like having poor three dimensional vision. Picture children attempting to catch a ball. When they have to adjust their position to catch, perhaps by moving their feet as well as stretching their arms and hands out to the side, the outcome is more likely to be successful if this is done in time to allow the hands to be positioned correctly. Children who are field independent see the approaching ball as distinct from the background early and so can judge when to move and where to move sooner than those who see it later. This explains why some children get flustered and try to catch after the ball has flown past – they did not see it coming in time to allow the necessary adjustments to be made.

Vision also plays a huge part in maintaining balance which is a central component of both movement and stillness. Any visual difficulty can mean that balance and therefore effective and efficient movement is very difficult. The simple act of walking forwards, heel to toe with eyes closed can prove this – if you doubt it, try!

Visual difficulties may cause children to avoid activities which require them to look out into space. Without help, their range of activities could be limited. It is also important to remember that the visual apparatus does not operate in isolation from the other senses. Goddard (1996) emphasizes that a rapid exchange of information passes between the vestibular apparatus, the eyes and the reflex response to incoming stimuli, and she shows how any defect in any of these systems will affect the smooth operation of the whole.

Those with visual difficulties may suffer

- problems in identifying letters and objects clearly
- inability to read without missing lines
- poor tracking skills
- distractibility, keeping them off task
- difficulty in precise movements
- poorly presented work
- having letters move or blur on the page
- becoming tired and frustrated after struggling to focus.

### Visual distractibility

Some children are too readily distracted by things happening in the environment around them. They have difficulty concentrating because the leaves on the tree flutter or children passing outside entice them to look away. They need a quiet space and activities which motivate them so that they stay focussed. Some children prefer to work facing a wall in the classroom because they recognize the difficulties they have keeping on task. Privacy makes them feel secure, but of course this move might upset other children and no one would wish them to feel different or isolated, so for them a quiet spot near the teacher, but beside friends is best.

## Proprioceptive/kinesthetic senses

The proprioceptive/kinesthetic senses provide information about where the body is in space and where the body parts are in relation to one another. They control spatial orientation or how effectively and efficiently movement happens in different environments. Proprioception involves all the sensations to do with position when the body is at rest while the kinesthetic sense comes into play when muscle contraction, i.e. movement, is part of the equation. Proprioceptors are all over the body – in muscles and joints and all over the skin. They function when the body is at rest and when adjustments in position have to be made. When movements need to be carried out without looking, e.g. sitting down on a chair, they can happen smoothly because the proprioceptors in the legs and hips tell the height of the seat and the distance the hips are from it. Some children with inefficient proprioceptive development have to turn and look and perhaps feel where the seat of the chair is and this takes time. These children can have problems with depth perception too and so hesitate in stepping from the kerb, or climb or go up and down stairs with much less confidence than their peers.

Those who find sitting or standing still difficult may have reduced proprioceptive input. This results in them having to move to get information from their kinesthetic sense. Information from both these senses, along with other sensory input, is processed through the vestibular sense, so any deficits there will impact on the proprioceptive/kinesthetic ones too. Children need to be able to use their eyes and ears and sense of balance along with their proprioceptive/kinesthetic senses if they are to be efficient and effective movers.

The proprioceptive and kinesthetic senses also impact on body image and body boundary. The body image is the picture children build of themselves through interpreting how others view them. If they are clumsy because their proprioceptors have given them faulty information, then others may deride their attempts and their self-esteem suffers. Their body boundary is the part where the skin meets the outside world and some children have great difficulty feeling where that is. This means that manipulating implements such as a knife and fork can be difficult – or swinging a bat or racquet or holding a frying pan, i.e. all manipulative actions which use tools. Again this results in poorly executed movement patterns which are open to public scrutiny. They may not risk repeated failure by trying again, so it is imperative that the children's difficulties are recognized and helped.

Those with proprioceptive/kinesthetic difficulties may suffer

- poor posture, low muscle tone
- constant restlessness
- bumping and barging due to poor spatial orientation
- balance difficulties leading to avoidance of activities.

## Taste and smell

The senses of taste and smell provide information about the kind of environment which surrounds the body. They also provide associated clues which determine action. A fresh leafy smell conjures up pictures of the countryside, spells out freedom and encourages running and jumping, while fog in the city tastes and smells horrible and indicates that indoors, huddled in a chair is a more comfortable place to be.

Smells can also stimulate the appetite. What hungry person can resist the smell of freshly baked bread and pass by on the other side? However, smells can conjure up unpleasant reminders too, e.g. the smell of dusty chalk can fill those who disliked school with dismay or the smell of disinfectant can bring back memories of visits to the hospital or to the vet with a favourite pet. Sometimes there is no explanation for children's low tolerance of smells – bathroom sprays, hair sprays, perfumes of any kind can produce what would seem to be an over-the-top reaction to those of us who are fortunate enough not to be hypersensitive.

At the other end of the scale are children who relish tastes and smells designed to put them off, e.g. the pills and potions which are free from flavours that children like, yet some seem to enjoy them despite the awful taste or smell. Accidents with children swallowing weed killers or other poisons still happen despite the taste and smell being ghastly to most adults. Obviously they have not been a sufficient deterrent to put the children off.

Those with taste/smell difficulties may suffer

- over-sensitivity to smells causing them to avoid places and people who 'smell'
- reactions to other children who sit close by
- food fads because the smell/taste is disagreeable
- severe illnesses through eating pills and medicines.

## Summary

As all of the senses work together, if one is inefficient then all of them will have some level of disadvantage. Too little input from any one may cause the child to appear poorly motivated, lacking interest and unwilling to sustain effort to complete a task, while too much may cause overactivity, overreaction and possible stress.

To help, adults must observe children in different environments to identify any stress factors (which should then be eliminated) and then compare their responses when they are relaxed and at ease. Such observations show how children see, what they hear, how they move and how they react to being touched. Important cues come from their willingness to touch others or their inability to stop, what they will wear, what they smell and generally how they use their senses to cope with the demands of their day. Poor sensory integration hinders both movement and learning. It is certainly critically important that adults understand how and take steps to help.

# Chapter 4

# Understanding co-occurrent difficulties

## Cognition, literacy and social communication

Part 1: Attention; memory; planning; organizing and sequencing; difficulty following instructions; poor concept of time; inconsistencies in performance.

Part 2: Literacy difficulties and phonological awarenes; language development.

Part 3: Social communication; making friends.

## Part 1

### Attention

> Case study 11
>
> Jamie, aged ten, had been two terms at his new school and his parents were anxiously awaiting his first report, hoping to hear that he had settled down well, made friends and that he was progressing with his studies. The report did say that Jamie was a pleasant, popular boy but that his attention was poor and his progress was slow. Comments such as 'easily distracted' came in each curricular area. Advice urging him to 'concentrate on his tasks' so that more of his work was completed was given more than once. Jamie's difficulty when asked to recall key facts from previous lessons and his unease when he was asked questions in class was noted. His teacher considered that 'Jamie should be doing better'. Jamie's parents were anxious to understand his difficulties so that they could plan the best ways to help. The first step appeared to be the need to pay attention.

Older children require persistence and attention over longer periods of time than younger ones do, so although 5- or 6-year-olds may well have been identified as being inattentive, this difficulty may not have caused too much concern. But if by age seven or eight children cannot concentrate, this significantly affects their achievement and so specific support is required. Many young children alternate periods of concentration with daydreaming or social chat, but they make up lost time by periods of intense concentration so they catch up and all is well. Others don't manage to do this. They stay distracted or unfocussed and the work just doesn't get done. Very often these children 'have the ability to do it', so it is not difficult to understand the frustration of everyone concerned, not least the children themselves, when reports continue to be disappointing.

### Inattention/distractibility can be due to a perceptual difficulty

Many children can concentrate when movement or noise surrounds them. They can cut out extraneous distractions and stay focussed on the task at hand, in fact some claim that they can only concentrate in the midst of noise! But there are children whose over-sensitivity causes them to look up from their work. They lose their thought process as well as their place and by the time they find it again, something else has moved or squeaked and so it goes on. When this is really troublesome and the children are constantly distracted, they are said to have an attention deficit disorder (ADD).

Another possibility is that the children are hyperactive, i.e. they have a hyper-kinetic syndrome, ADHD (attention deficit hyperactivity disorder). They cannot resist the urge to move, their work is delayed – this time because they are out of their seat rearranging things or checking that everyone else is busy. One theory is that these children require constant movement to tell them where they are in space – their proprioceptors (nerve endings in the muscles) needing constant feedback from the environment so that they can feel stable and in control. Many children with dyspraxia exhibit this restlessness, but much less severely than children with ADHD.

Barkley (1990) writes about children with ADHD. He explains that in a busy environment, these children 'are unable to inhibit their reactions to all the sights and sounds around them' and their response is constant movement. In fact their activity is so 'strikingly different, that even novice observers have no difficulty in picking out children with ADHD' (Bee 1999). The difference is shown when children without the condition are motivated to be still, for when they are really interested they can concentrate and complete their work. Perhaps they don't always oblige, but that is quite different from children who just can't be still. Moreover, about half the children with ADHD will talk, not only out of turn, but also out of context so that their interruptions only serve to annoy. Some show aggression and have difficulty making friends because they do not understand the other child's social cues. This makes them different from other groups. It is important therefore to distinguish between children who have a hyperactivity disorder (ADHD) and those who don't pay attention, i.e. those with ADD (attention deficit disorder), or those who are just disobeying a plea to 'keep still' because they would much prefer to be doing something else. The attention disorders can last into adolescence and adulthood (half to three-quarters of all cases do), the worst combination being when ADHD is combined with aggression (Munden and Arcelus 1999). (The criteria for identifying ADHD are in the Appendix.)

## What is involved in paying attention?

As young people develop, they learn to control the way in which they stay with a task and they accumulate strategies which could be helpful in solving it. With experience of earlier tasks, they increasingly recognize the length of time/the depth of scrutiny/the alternative ways they might approach each task and they select – more or less appropriately – from a range of possibilities. So paying attention is much more than 'being still'. It requires

- sufficient general ability to understand the demands of the task
- recall of previous experience and learning
- recognition of various strategies and selection of the right one
- self-control to stay with the task until it is completed.

Some children with specific learning difficulties may need help to enable them to pay attention. They may not naturally direct their gaze to things that are being shown or demonstrations that are taking place. Some can do so if they are directed to 'look there' or 'follow that path' but they don't do this intuitively because of their difficulty relating emotionally to what others do. Many children with Asperger's syndrome are like this. Despite being near at hand and having colourful, lively demonstrations so that they can use their visual sense (a strength in many children), teachers can't assume that the children will be motivated or be able to watch what is going on.

Some children, however, will be paying intense attention even though they are not watching. This can complicate assessments. They can be listening actively, but because they are not following the teacher's non-verbal cues, they give the impression that they are not paying attention. Nonetheless they are learning – in fact they may be extremely anxious to complete their work to a high standard, using much energy and enthusiasm, even obsession to do so. To save intervening unnecessarily and misguidedly, the staff have to observe the children's responses very carefully. It is not easy to do this and mistakes can cause real hurt and confusion.

### Case study 12

Diane, a class teacher of five-year-olds, called the children to the front to begin identifying the first letters in their names. Harry remained firmly in his seat. Neither Diane nor the other children enticed him to come forward. As the lesson progressed, Harry continued his writing on a piece of paper, but when he was asked if a particular letter was 'his one' he responded correctly, obviously following the lesson and learning from it. To an outsider it might have appeared that the child was not paying attention, yet the teacher and the children recognized that Harry preferred not to join the group, allowed this 'accommodation' and were shown that he was participating as well as any other child in the class.

### Gaining attention

The other side of giving attention is gaining attention and some children have not the confidence to make their requests known – they may be nervous that their peers will overhear and pass some scathing comment or be afraid that any response will raise more difficulties. For whatever reason they choose to be silent, while at the same time being aware that this is not a strategy which leads to success.

On the other hand there are some children who do not understand how to communicate with other people because they do not appreciate the underlying requirements, e.g. that there must be someone there to listen. Jordan and Powell (1995) tell of a child who repeated a message she had practised to an empty room, 'the fact that the Secretary was not there was of no significance to her'. This child who had Asperger's syndrome had yet to appreciate that there needs to be an audience for messages to be conveyed successfully.

Then again there are some children who gain attention in a totally inappropriate manner, perhaps by hitting the person whose attention they wish to attract or shouting out at quite the wrong time. Not understanding how the recipient will feel or react, they can be amazed by the kind of retaliation they receive. Games in the hall which involve gentle touching to pass on messages can help children, especially those with Asperger's syndrome or dyspraxia, to gauge the strength and the kind of communication that is appropriate. Parents and staff have to understand that 'pay attention' is not the simplistic command that one would imagine. The children's difficulties have to be understood in detail through careful observation so that teachers can anticipate confrontations and do their best to avert them.

There are also temporary and external reasons why paying attention could be problematic. Illness and tiredness certainly influence concentration so that learning is impaired, as does some medication. Stress from upsets at home also impinge upon the children's day and who can blame them for not attending to a lesson when they are visualizing upheavals at home which are going to affect them profoundly and cause their family distress?

### Strategies for support

- Many children with specific learning difficulties need to be shown how to read non-verbal cues. They have difficulty interpreting facial expressions, especially more subtle cues such as disgust or withdrawal. How to do this may need to be explained on lots of different occasions, possibly by showing carefully selected pictures and then by having fun interactions where the children have to demonstrate through facial expressions that they are angry or afraid or happy. Once some success has been gained then having the same expressions in different contexts can help children appreciate transfer of learning from one situation to another, e.g. Mum looks cross when juice is spilt all over the floor – the lollipop man looks cross when children run into the road. The next stage would be to have the children make up episodes or stories of people showing different emotions and eventually some of the children would be able to engage in role-play.

- If the children are easily distracted, then encourage them to sit in a quiet spot, facing away from windows but not isolated from the other children. They should have an uninterrupted view of the chalkboard when teaching is conducted there even if this means temporarily leaving their seat. Sitting beside a child who provides a good role model sometimes helps them to stay calm.
- Catch them 'paying attention' and give immediate praise (this may be a smile and a nod or a more public 'Well done', depending on the preferences of the child).
- Ignore minor behaviour lapses whenever possible and when some admonition is necessary, then ensure that the children know that it is the behaviour not themselves as people that is causing the concern.
- Intersperse activity with sitting and listening sessions. Allow those who find keeping still difficult to lean on a support or use a beanbag to absorb some of their movement. A ball of clay to mould can let them move their hands as they listen. This often helps concentration.
- Include oral assessment as much as possible so that children who find staying with a writing task difficult have a genuine chance to shine.
- Some staff have found that arranging a private, 'secret' signal, such as a child placing a pencil sharpener at a prearranged spot on the desk, works well. This indicates that the child needs attention. Others have asked the children to put a special mark in their jotter; others have given a sympathetic, responsible child who is willing to help, a 'helping hand' role.
- The children have to have a clear picture of what the task involves. This may mean that instructions have to be repeated more than once, preferably using different phrases if comprehension is difficult. A visual representation, i.e. a picture or model can usefully accompany verbal instructions.
- Give the whole picture for those who learn holistically, then break the task down into smaller stages for those with limited attention.
- Playing classical music, especially Mozart, is calming for many children.

When young people fail to pay attention, their difficulties might not be in distractibility or in using an impulsive learning style. They could need help to understand the task itself, reminders of the organizational demands, encouragement that they can manage or ongoing subtle reminders to stay still. Above all they need to believe that they can cope and that they are progressing.

## Memory

Many children with specific learning difficulties find memorizing problematic. This is particularly the case with the short term/working memory. In a mathematics workbook where the instructions are written at the top of the page, children who have working memory difficulties may continue down the line of sums forgetting the instruction to subtract and end up adding the numbers together. They can manage the technique, but 'get marked wrong' because they forget the instructions. If the children forget the mathematical symbols, a difficulty which particularly affects children with dyslexia, then confusion is made worse.

Remembering is obviously a fundamental requisite of learning, especially as new learning almost invariably involves some kind of comparison to what has gone before. Even saying something like 'I've never seen one like that before', involves some kind of comparison of the features of the new to the old, i.e. to something stored in the memory. This hunting for similarities and differences is a fundamental part of categorizing the new alongside the old.

There are many young people who find great difficulty in remembering. When some are asked questions about recent events, e.g. 'What did you do in school today?' they often answer 'nothing' to the surprise and frustration of the teacher as well as the parent. Is this because the children have not the language to explain? Or in a thematic approach to teaching where the subjects blend into one another, has the removal of barriers between subjects denied the children the means to identify what they were doing? Or is there some neurological deficit which makes recent recall problematic?

### Case study 13

Craig, an 11-year-old, suspected of having dyslexia and dyspraxia, happily and immediately told me that his school lunches were 'rubbish' but looked blank and couldn't remember when asked at 2 p.m. what he had had for lunch that day! When he was prompted by a statement, 'I used to like school soup best' (not another question which could have perplexed him), he was able to recall that he hadn't had soup that day. 'We didn't get pea soup or tomato but sometimes we do ... but not today'. He didn't volunteer any more information but seemed very pleased to have remembered something. Perhaps the questioner has to be sensitive and break down the range of recall which is being asked, i.e. not about lunches generally in this instance, but about just one part, the soup course. Howe (1989) explains that retrieval processes like this may be more problematic for children who experience difficulties in learning.

Memory can be particularly selective in children with Asperger's syndrome. Some children have a prodigious memory for facts and details of events but no recall of personal involvement. They may tell about their school, its history, how many children are in the different classes, the buses which pass the door, yet not proffer any information about how they themselves participated in any way, even whether they were happy or disappointed or felt left out. While they could recall facts as semantics, they were not aware of how they felt about personal episodes, i.e. they showed very poor autobiographical memory. This meant that remembering was not aided by being able to store emotional events, often the very skills that stimulate recall.

Meadows (1993) explains that the development of memory from childhood to adulthood should have four aspects,

1    an improvement in basic capacities such as memory size or the speed of basic memory processes
2    development of more sophisticated memory strategies allowing diversity and flexibility
3    changes in 'metamemory', i.e. children's understanding and awareness of how they use their memories
4    more generalized knowledge which could make remembering related situations easier.

## Strategies to help memorizing

• Rehearsal
• Organization
• Building expert knowledge.

### REHEARSAL

'Rehearsal' is simply repeating items that are to be remembered – usually quickly with intense concentration. This strategy suffices for items which have to be remembered for a brief time till they are written down or can be forgotten, e.g. telephone numbers. In addition, repeated rehearsal helps people remember things which need quick recall, e.g. 'rules' such as 'i' before 'e' except after 'c', or times tables which are rote learned possibly without any real understanding of what the different figures or the signs mean. Certainly mnemonics can be retrieved from the stored memory years after they have been learned – often without any recall of what they stood for! Quick recall needs to be tested in context before comprehension can be assumed; however, there are times when just finding an answer can be enough, e.g. in coping with basic shopping. So, while rote learning is often dismissed as surface learning, it can give a boost to children who find recall problematic.

### ORGANIZATION

A second strategy to help memorizing is organization. This involves categorizing the separate items by group names so that, for example, 'fruit' replaces a list of oranges, apples and plums. The one remembered name can then spur the memory to recall the detailed list. Buzan (1993) recommends that children compile a visual picture – a mind map accompanied by a story to help them remember. Recalling the picture, he claims, can stimulate the memory to help recall of what the named objects within the picture stood for.

Children, especially younger ones, may need examples as to how this can be done. It is worth the effort, because although the active short-term memory usually only holds seven numbers or words in a list, if one of these is cumulative, e.g. 'the things I need for my school project', then the amount of information held can be considerably increased. The visualization of a folder containing all these items would also ease remembering for some children.

Similarly, timetables, checklists and organizer trays – one for each day of the week – can reduce the number of items to be remembered and let the children concentrate on the task at hand.

## BUILDING EXPERT KNOWLEDGE

All of these strategies are helped by expert knowledge about the topic which is held in the memory. This being so, increasing the memory of details can come through building up background knowledge.

*Examples*  Young people who have grown up with football, as just one example, are more likely to be able to memorize then recall new game plans because they have existing knowledge and so can compare the old with the new. They can 'see' the proposed pattern of play because they already know about the rules, the techniques and the tactics which are part of the basic game.

How could this help other children with poor short-term memories? Perhaps taking young people to the theatre could help children with communication difficulties, because there they see different modes of interaction in duo form. The child is the onlooker and has the opportunity to see both sides in action, to hear how clearly and how expressively the words have to be spoken and to appreciate the distance between the speakers as the different sorts of interchange (confiding, confrontational, beseeching, repelling) take place. For many children the point of this would have to be spelled out. In addition, the theme of the play could be discussed in terms of the feelings of the characters, so encouraging empathy without the child being personally involved. This kind of discussion can happen without any stress or feeling of 'having to get it right'.

In a pantomime the use of non-verbal communication is often overstressed which makes the meaning more accessible to children who do not interpret expressions readily. As the mother in *Jack and the Beanstalk* shows her anger with Jack for selling the cow for beans, she is likely to be thumping the table or strutting around waving her arms, thus gesturing to show her displeasure. And when Cinderella finds she can't go to the ball, her posture as she cries will show sadness. It is vitally important that adults recognize opportunities to develop the children's ability to interpret non-verbal cues in this kind of way. This involves analyzing the learning potential of each experience in line with the kinds of difficulties the young people have and taking time to explain reasons why certain ways of behaving occurred.

Taking children to climb hills and look down on their city or on the different levels of fields and rivers can help them appreciate what three-dimensional mapping really involves. Seeing a reservoir can help children appreciate the volume of water held there and make a lesson on the distribution of water to houses more meaningful. Close inspection of the hedgerows can let them appreciate the different homes that are built there and make environmental issues come alive. Keeping learning active need not be totally down to the school staff. Many parents would like to be involved if they were helped to understand the kind of interaction which would be the most helpful; they would, of course, have to realize that many of the children have to be helped to observe and make connections between experiences.

Every experience has the potential to help 'remembering' and by understanding how to help the children process, retain, then recall and 'use' the information, adults can boost both their self-esteem and their achievement. Specific knowledge can lead to more 'expert' ways of processing understanding and solving problems. Perhaps parents could discuss forward planning with the teacher and so boost the child's related general knowledge about the forthcoming topic so that references within the lesson could be assimilated more easily.

### Planning, organizing and sequencing

One of the common frustrations for children is to do with their planning and organizing skills. Basic everyday tasks such as getting dressed can still be time-consuming and confusing even for 10- and 11-year-olds. Having problems remembering where things are, even though they were in use a moment ago, leads to lots of frustration. Constantly having to refer to timetables instead of instantly recalling when things are to happen or forgetting to take a bus pass or PE equipment to school – all of these sorts of difficulties arise when planning and organizing is problematic. One way to help is to analyze the actions which are causing the difficulties and point out ways to solve them, e.g. that in tying laces, making a firm knot first saves retaining the tension of the two laces while the bow is made. Another good way to help is to have quite a rigid routine so that most of the day's events can be anticipated. Timetables are invaluable, provided of course that the children remember to use them and 'someone' – preferably an adult – takes the responsibility of updating them and pointing out changes to the children who have planning difficulties.

At the micro level, the planning implicit within tasks can be very difficult too. Knowing how to organize sequences within an imaginative story or a movement sequence in the gym, even remembering rules of a game and recognizing the differences when the teams change ends – all of these kinds of actions need careful and repeated explanations if the knowledge base is not to be distorted by poor sequencing skills.

The most helpful strategy is having a strict routine and only gradually easing changes into the programme. All sorts of checklists can be brought into use to take away the stress of having to remember. Ticking off achievements as they are accomplished can help the youngsters to appreciate the logic of the event.

Asking children to order a sequence of pictures about events in the day or well-known stories can help staff appreciate whether the children understand concepts such as 'before', or 'afterwards', 'sooner' or 'later'. Many children, particularly those with SLI, could use these words without really getting to grips with their meaning.

### Strategies to support

Everyone finds retention of material easier if it is of interest because then it is more meaningful. New learning is more easily retained if it is not too distant from the old so that the learning demands are not too great (the memory store will contain things which have been meaningful to the child and these can be used for comparison and extension). Yet there are other things which must be learned if meeting targets is on the agenda and sometimes, and very sadly, these can be of little interest and too far removed from the children's existing knowledge to be readily retained in the memory. This often leads to children 'shutting off' and withdrawing from the learning experience in some way. Schools have recognized this and taken some measures to overcome it. Differentiating the curriculum has helped. Children with difficulties are having work matched to their specific learning needs and so are enabled to experience success.

### Difficulty following instructions

Children with auditory sequential memory difficulties will be unable to follow a series of instructions. Often they stand looking at the teacher after a sequence of instructions has been given. In some cases the children are simply processing the information which has been given. Time is required for this processing to take place. Often, as the information is processed, some is forgotten so the children may remember only the last instruction and do only that one. A teacher who does not understand the difficulties the children are having may become exasperated and cause them to feel inadequate or confused.

It is important for teachers to remember that children with specific learning difficulties process information more slowly than their peer group. Time must be given for this processing. Processing difficulties can be compounded by the teacher's rate of speech. Children respond better to a moderate rate of speech and can become confused when the rate is too fast.

### Poor concept of time

Many children with specific learning difficulties have a poor concept of time. Children may leave the class at lunchtime with their schoolbag, ready to go home.

This is not necessarily an indication that the morning has dragged, rather confirmation that they have a poor awareness of time. This may result in their being late for school, late home or late for any clubs or activities. It is easy to see why parents, teachers and the children themselves become upset. Ensuring that children have watches doesn't solve the problem. Watches can warn that school begins in ten minutes, but children with a poor concept of time may consider that ten minutes is sufficient to get there when it is not.

### Inconsistencies in performance: open and closed skills

'Performance' is very often inconsistent in children with specific learning difficulties and understandably this causes frustration to the children and the adults who have been supporting them. The cause may be that the context requires a different kind of skill, i.e. an open skill rather than a closed one.

### Case study 14

Jessica and her teacher were delighted that she had mastered her spelling words and got full marks in a test. Immediately after, however, she was unable to use the same words correctly in a piece of imaginative writing and became distressed when this was pointed out. Both the teacher and the child were perplexed by this inability to use the words in a different context.

WHAT WAS WRONG?

In the first instance, i.e. at the test, only one skill was called on, i.e. spelling the word correctly. In the second, however, many more competencies were required. The idea for the story had to be created, suitable vocabulary selected, the order of words had to be considered, and both correct punctuation and correct spelling had to be remembered. Although the words could be correctly spelt in isolation, i.e. as a closed skill, when spelling in context, i.e. as an open skill, the child was overwhelmed.

### Case study 15

Struan was very anxious to be in the school football team and to achieve this, he practised shooting goals every evening until his aim was accurate and goals were scored. He was confident that he would gain a place in the team. How disappointed he was to discover that in the turbulence of the game, his skill disappeared and he fluffed each attempt to score. While he had been able to shoot accurately as a closed skill, i.e. when the environmental demands were few, he was unable to transfer his skill to the changing context of the game. He was unable to attend to more than one thing at a time.

### Strategies to help

If children find difficulty in coping with complex tasks, teachers need to recognize how the contextual demands influence the skills that are required. In addition they could:

- encourage the children to proofread their work carefully. This provides an opportunity to self-correct spelling errors. At this stage, the other demands of writing task, i.e. imagining, planning and sequencing, are removed and the spelling becomes a closed skill once more.
- reduce the environmental demands – the football game, as one example, could be built up from a pairs game with one shooter and one in goal, to a small-side game before the complexities of rules and positioning of the whole game were introduced.
- give visual clues, e.g. a list of reminders or a picture which contained helpful hints, or provide concrete materials, e.g. word banks or actual artifacts to spur the memory of earlier work so that recall is eased.
- encourage overlearning, because as skills become consolidated, there is more chance of them becoming habitual or automatic.

### Summary

Keeping instructions to a minimum; giving them one at a time until the children can cope with more; augmenting verbal instructions by visual cues; explaining clearly and not taking for granted that seemingly straightforward instructions are understood can all be helpful. It must be recognized, however, that some children will always find it impossible to retain a series of instructions and respond appropriately.

## Part 2

### Literacy difficulties

#### Reading

Reading is an interactive process which involves the synthesis of auditory, visual, and contextual factors. Successful and rapid synthesis leads to successful comprehension, so if decoding is slow and laboured comprehension is compromised. A point of breakdown can be reached during this process.

## Phonological awareness

There are several reasons why children may experience difficulties acquiring literacy skills. In the case of children with dyslexia and/or SLI, poor phonological awareness is often implicated. Children who have phonological difficulties may experience difficulty with:

- grapheme/phoneme correspondence
- blending
- segmentation
- rhyme and analogy.

Each of the sub-skills of reading can be problematic for children. The increased recognition that some sub-skills must be taught in the nursery/early primary days has helped to consolidate these skills at the pre-reading stage rather than teachers having to return to them further up the school in order to 'remediate'. The advent of the Literacy Hour has resulted in many excellent publications addressing phonological awareness and it is now seen as an important prerequisite to the acquisition of literacy skills. However, appreciating the child's stage of reading readiness might mean that more preparatory work has to be done.

## Visual aspects

### LEFT–RIGHT ORIENTATION

Left–right orientation is not firmly established in some young readers. In these cases tracking tasks or 'joining the dots' left to right can be helpful exercises. These, however, must be supervised otherwise the children may resort to a right–left preference.

### POOR VISUAL MEMORY

A poor visual memory can result in the slow acquisition of sight vocabulary. Children experiencing difficulty here will need much overlearning in as many different ways as possible, for example using sideways extension books (which offer opportunities for consolidation without introducing new vocabulary) and playing games using the key words to consolidate their basic sight vocabulary.

### VISUAL DISTURBANCE

### Case study 16

Stephanie was at the end of her first year at school. She had good communication skills and was clearly interested in all that was going on in class. She was, however, making slow progress with her reading. Investigation of her Baseline Assessment results revealed no particular difficulty with phonological awareness and a more focussed investigation confirmed that Stephanie was able to select the correct word when asked to find the odd one out in a list of rhyming words. She could also supply rhyming words when asked. What was amiss? Stephanie's teacher discussed the problem with a learning support teacher who visited the class to watch her at work and read with her. She asked Stephanie to tell her what she saw when she looked at the page. Stephanie said the letters 'moved on the page'. Different coloured overlays were placed over the page until a pale blue was chosen 'because that was the one which made the letters stay still'. The visual disturbance which occurred when Stephanie looked at print was reduced.

Visual disturbance can result from an impaired magnocellular system, which Stein (2001) claim can lead to binocular instability, causing letters to appear to move or cross over each other. The problem with young readers is that they are not aware that what they see is different to what others see.

There are other forms of visual disturbance which can cause problems in learning to read. Some children are affected by glare. Black print on a white background jumps and flickers, therefore reading books, looking at chalkboards or whiteboards can cause real difficulty. Coloured overlays are clearly only helpful when reading books so another solution must be found to help board work. This comes in the form of spectacles with tinted lenses which reduce glare and generally calm things down. The children select the most effective tint when an ophthalmic optician who specializes in this difficulty undertakes an assessment.

Justified print can also be problematic for some children who benefit more from the even spacing of words. Reading books, which avoid the use of justified print and black print on white paper, are now being published especially for children who experience visual disturbance. Barrington Stoke Publications supply texts like this (available from 10 Belford Terrace, Edinburgh).

## Comprehension

The purpose of reading is to understand the meaning of words. Dyslexic pupils who struggle to decode print often amaze teachers when they are able to discuss what they have read. Some children have the opposite problem because they have absolutely no difficulty decoding and could be described as fluent readers, but questioning finds that they have little or no understanding of what has been read. Teachers describe such pupils as 'barking at print'. A more technical term is 'hyperlexic'. The way forward in this situation is to slow the children down as they read, encouraging them to think about the meaning in the text. An exercise which involves blanking out the occasional word and so encouraging speculation as to what it may be, is a useful strategy to slow the children down and encourage better comprehension.

## Writing

There are complex skills and sub-skills involved in writing. This explains why so many children have difficulties. Writing involves the sub-skills of:

- organization of ideas
- letter formation
- spelling
- punctuation.

Each of these sub-skills demands a particular cognitive function. Both the organizations of ideas and letter formation benefit from visual imagery. Spelling involves word retrieval and punctuation involves memory. These sub-skills must come together if children are to be successful writers. If the complications of poor muscle tone, awkward pencil grip, posture, hand-eye coordination and difficulties in crossing the midline are added to this, the surprise should be the numbers of children who experience little difficulty.

## Spelling

Here again, difficulties can be due to the auditory or visual aspects of spelling or a combination of the two. Children who have difficulty decoding usually have difficulty encoding. The teaching of spelling involves two different types of words: those which are described as irregular words, and those which fit into a pattern or sequence. Some spelling books present words with similar patterns which 'sound' the same, for example 'fight, sight, might', but children who have auditory difficulties may not hear the similarity and may end up learning each word separately. The use of onset and rime helps to highlight the pattern. The 'onset' is made up of the initial consonant or consonants and the rime is made up of the vowel and remaining consonants. As an example 'sight' and 'fight' have the onsets 's' and 'f' but share the same rime 'ight'. Writing the words vertically helps children to see the pattern and makes learning easier. Children who have visual difficulties, however, may not remember the pattern of words. This could be helped by boxing the letters (see Figure 4.1). Practising fitting letters into blank boxes (shaped to accommodate the letter), is a fun activity for children and a good way of over-learning, especially for irregular key words, as it helps to establish the visual pattern.

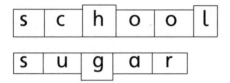

*Figure 4.1* Shapes of words

## Difficulties with language development

Language development is one of the most important areas of development in pre-school children. Some children demonstrate considerable difficulties in this area. Children whose language development follows the usual pathway demonstrate age-appropriate skills within the various components of language, i.e. phonology, vocabulary, grammar and pragmatics. However, children with a language impairment have difficulty with one or more than one of these components. Within the four components of language children may experience a difficulty with either comprehension or expression or both.

Indicators of phonological difficulties may be reflected in auditory discrimination difficulties, as in children with dyslexia, or difficulty with the motor planning for speech, as in children with verbal dyspraxia. There may also be difficulty with pronunciation. Children with vocabulary difficulties may have difficulties with comprehension, especially with more abstract vocabulary. They may have a word finding difficulty, as children with dyslexia, and may use long descriptions because they cannot find a single required word. Some children have a difficulty with grammar and this may be reflected in their understanding of speech and text and in their expression with the use of short, simple sentences. Finally, some children have difficulty with pragmatics, especially where idioms are used. As an example, a child who is asked to draw the curtains (because the sun is shining through a window behind) may actually pick up a pencil and draw a pair of curtains. It is easy to see how a genuine language difficulty can lead to children being accused of being smart or cheeky.

The above difficulties can exist separately or they may co-occur. Clearly, the more co-occurrence, the more complicated the language impairment. Children whose difficulties lie more with their expressive vocabulary are usually easier to identify, although they may simply be considered to be quiet children. However, children whose difficulties are more with the comprehension of speech may not be so easy to identify, and their problems are often not appreciated by parents or teachers. Children may be accused of being lazy or disobedient when they are neither. The difficulty is that they are having problems processing language. By the time a sentence has been processed children may already be in trouble for not having responded immediately.

Children are considered to have a specific language impairment (SLI) when there is a discrepancy between the verbal and non-verbal scores in a standardized assessment and where such difficulties are not related to any hearing impairment. Children have a difficulty communicating their needs or preferences and this difficulty is usually evident before attending school. Clearly, early diagnosis is desirable and possible and support from a speech and language therapist is necessary.

Difficulties with language development invariably affect progress with literacy skills. It is therefore important that teachers are aware that some children may be experiencing difficulty in this area and that teachers ensure their teaching styles are supportive.

Strategies to support expressive language difficulties:

- encourage interactions with a small group of children
- encourage role play, again within a small group
- praise correct/appropriate use of speech.

Strategies to support comprehension difficulties:

- use a multisensory approach to teaching, offering hands on experience where possible
- ensure children have understood a request/instruction before expecting them to comply
- offer a demonstration if possible
- speak clearly
- speak slowly
- use visual cues
- modify text if necessary by highlighting/adding diagrams.

## Part 3

### Social communication: making friends

Everyone hopes that children at school will be happy and for most this means that they will have friends. Sadly, however, some children with specific learning difficulties find they are left alone. Although there are those who prefer this as they find people coming close stressful, most would love to be able to sustain friendships and be part of a group. To make matters worse many teachers feel unable to help, not understanding how to help their children to make friends.

What then are the competencies that are helpful in making friends? Children must

- have the confidence to approach other children or to welcome them as friends
- be able to hold eye contact so that others do not feel rebuffed
- be able to read non-verbal cues and respond appropriately
- be able to pretend and to understand another child's pretence
- be able to wait and take turns in conversations and at play
- be able to follow someone else's lead or the rules of the game

- be able to make the correct response – neither too timid nor too aggressive
- be able to empathise with another's distress
- have the skills to participate in the chosen activities.

Comparing these competencies to the difficulties implicit in some specific learning conditions shows how problematic it is for children who have them to make and retain friends.

When 'poor communication' is raised as an issue, many people think of children on the autistic spectrum and indeed the triad of impairments listed by Wing and Gould (1979) explain such children display, among other difficulties, a lack of empathy with the perceptions of others and little understanding of give and take. They also tend to avoid eye contact which can cause children offering friendship to feel rebuffed. Children with other learning difficulties suffer too. Children with ADD may not manage to concentrate to discover the plot of a game while those with ADHD may not be able to wait to see the game plan unfold. Those with dyspraxia may not have the coordination or movement skills to let them join in and especially if a group is chosen, they are likely to be omitted from the cast. It is not difficult to understand how such rejections cause deep hurt, even though some children may assert that they don't care. Such frustrations can easily lead to aggression and this in turn causes further isolation.

## Strategies to help

### SHARING AN INTEREST

Bee (1999) suggests that those who wish to promote friendships among children should identify the activities that those with difficulties like to do. In this way the children are able to participate, even play a central role in developments, for their prior experience stands them in good stead, helping them to appreciate what is going on. She then suggests that other children with the same interests, no matter whether the parents think they are likely to be friends or not, are invited to join in. She asserts that it is the cooperation which results from interest in the activity rather than the children themselves, which makes the difference. The group has a shared commitment; a source of forward planning and a target for shared practice and increased skill. Bee claims that this is the surest route to friendship.

### HELPING CHILDREN TO UNDERSTAND EMOTIONS

Many children do not understand emotions and fail to appreciate how others feel. One reason is that they are unable to read the visual cues given through expressions and body language. This can be practised through games, e.g. 'Show me how you look if … someone takes your favourite cake … or you meet an alien … or you fall into sticky brown mud'. This may be taught as a group activity and when the idea is established, practised in twos, giving the children lots of fun in making and interpreting facial expressions. Once the picture is linked with the emotion, thoughts about subsequent actions can be added, e.g. 'Why is Liam crying? How can we make him feel better? How can we get help?'

Pictures in storybooks can stimulate simple understandings about emotions by asking, 'How are these children feeling? What do you think has made them happy? How would you feel if that happened to you?' This is an important strategy because only through recognizing emotions can children empathise with the feelings of others and anticipate what they are likely to do. They also need to be helped to recognize how they themselves would be likely to behave in an emotional situation and consider whether that was the best way.

## THOMAS THE TANK ENGINE

Young children love these videos which are a wonderful stimulus for explaining emotions. The sad engine chugs slowly along with a droopy mouth and puffing clouds of depressing grey smoke ... while the happy one chats to the others and smiles to them all. The stories stimulate good discussions because the children themselves haven't caused any of the hurt and are 'not to blame' for the engines' emotional states. For many children this makes a welcome change.

## INVADING PERSONAL SPACE

Although many children are overprotective of their own personal space, even hitting out if others encroach, many more have no idea that they are causing offence by invading other people's space and they can be devastated when they are pushed away, misinterpreting the action as a personal rejection. Many children with dyspraxia experience this. Explanations can usefully be reinforced by spatial awareness games which help recognition of distances, e.g. 'Run and stand quite near the wall without touching ... move further away – the length of your arm ... now move in closer ... look, there is a much smaller space now'. Lots of running and stopping near a partner, measuring the distance and then repeating the activity 'stopping further away' can help children appreciate the correct distances for encouraging conversations.

## TURN-TAKING

Children with ADHD may have difficulty waiting their turn while children with Asperger's syndrome may not recognize the pattern at all. Games such as peep-bo for the very young and Snakes and Ladders for the older ones can help children appreciate why turn-taking is important in establishing 'rules'.

## LEARNING TO PRETEND

Children with Asperger's syndrome can have difficulty pretending and understanding what others do or think when they pretend. This means they lose the sequence of events and fail to understand the logic of subsequent actions or conversations. Gradually introducing opportunities for role-play, e.g. being a 'Mum' or 'Dad' in the 'House' corner or acting out parts in favourite stories, can help this. In *Goldilocks and the Three Bears*, as one example, discussions about feelings can complement the role-play, e.g. 'How do you think Goldilocks felt when she woke up and saw Baby Bear?' Stewart (2002) is one teacher who tried this with children with Asperger's syndrome with some success. Her children learned to use the phrase, 'I'm pretending to be ...' and close observations showed that two of the three children in the group had understood what the concept meant.

## THE DEVELOPMENT OF ALTRUISM AND EMPATHY

Developing altruism, i.e. being willing to do a good turn at some cost to oneself, and empathy, i.e. understanding and sharing the feelings of another, is at the root of perception. If children don't understand how others see the world and so react to happenings in it, their own reactions and responses can be unexpected or cause hurt and dismay and lead to the child being left out of group activities. They need lots of explanations of simple events, e.g. 'John is crying because he has fallen and hurt his knee so we are helping him by saying how sorry we are'. Stories which ask children how they would respond in situations which could have different kinds of replies, can provide adults with insights as to whether these attributes have developed. Using other names can depersonalize the story and remove any feeling of 'having to get it right'.

One such story might be:

> Emma was on her way to meet her friends at a cafe for a special tea. On her way she found that an old lady had fallen over in the street. The lady was very upset. Emma knew that if she stopped to help, she would miss her tea. What should she do?

All of the strategies which have been suggested in this chapter are part of the challenge to find new ways of keeping children safe and making learning fun.

# Chapter 5

# Understanding co-occurrent difficulties

## Movement fluency, confused laterality, rhythm and timing

Learning to move is such an important part of growing up. Most very young children are not content to stay still but constantly set themselves movement challenges – to crawl, then walk, then run and jump – and all of these skills appear to give them pleasure and confidence to try again. Gradually they are able to increase the repertoire of movements which they habituate (do without consciously planning each step) and with practice they become able to alter them to suit the demands of different environments. Thus, running to meet Mum to have a hug can adapt to running in a game of tig in the playground, to dodging and marking on the sports field or combining running with jumping to score a basket or to jump on a bus. In this way, single actions which need planning and organizing become part of complex moves which involve apparatus or adjusting the action to comply with a different terrain. Luckily, young children try out lots of movements when they are being supervised by adults, although having said that there does seem to be an inbuilt safety mechanism in most children which prevents too many accidents!

Apart from its own intrinsic merit, being able to move confidently eases all different kinds of learning – intellectual learning, because so much of the curriculum is based on practical activities, e.g. drawing and writing. Movement underpins social learning too, because finding people who have the same sorts of interests is a sure way to make friends (Bee 1999). Being able to ride a bike lets children go off with their peer group and find new environments to explore. This gives them a time for independence when they can be responsible for themselves, free from adults looking over their shoulders. They also have some new experiences to talk about at home and in school. If they can catch a ball or kick a goal and remember rules, then they can get into a game and be part of a team. Unfortunately many children with specific learning difficulties lose out because they find such activities so difficult to do. They do learn to run and jump but not very well and riding a bike can be impossible.

Movement dexterity allows children to have leisure choices too. This means that hobbies, e.g. all kinds of art and craft work as well as those using gross motor skills, can be selected with confidence. Emotional learning is also helped, for just being in a crowd and having the ability to do what the others do is very gratifying for children, especially for those who may be unsure of their popularity. And in a group situation, other children provide role models of different ways of reacting and other ways of caring as well as giving examples of different coping strategies. All of these may provide pointers for reflection and possible modelling. Furthermore, because moving well gives confidence, this can transfer to tackling new activities with relish rather then being afraid to try. Achieving 'movement milestones', e.g. being able to tie laces, play football, ride a bike at the same time as their friends, is important for children and their parents. 'Not being able to match the norm' can be an early sign of specific learning difficulties.

Many children with specific learning difficulties do not follow the usual developmental pattern. There are five main 'movement' reasons why:

1    They have hypotonia or low muscle tone which means that they lack strength and control in their limbs. If this affects the shoulders, arms and wrists, activities such as writing, drawing, cutting out and carrying objects may be very difficult.
2    They have poorly developed body and spatial awareness and lack an accurate sense of body boundary. This means that they are unsure of exactly where their body parts are in relation to one another and where they are in relation to the objects around them. And when manipulative skills are required, difficulty in realizing where the body ends and the 'tool' begins means that 'picking up, handling and letting go' may all be compromised.
3    They have a poorly developed sense of rhythm and timing which affects their coordination. If the fluency of the movement is impaired as a result of this, momentum from one movement is not used to begin the next. More effort is needed and the movement appears as 'stop-start' or clumsy rather than flowing and easy.
4    They do not habituate their movements so each must be done as a first time try. Movements therefore appear unpractised and unskilled.
5    They take inaccurate cues from the environment which affects their decision making about distance and timing.

When difficulies are observed, words like 'awkward', 'jerky', 'tripping over thin air', 'cumbersome', 'ungainly' and 'uncoordinated' spring to mind. The first indicators are likely to be poor coordination, balance, body awareness, rhythm and timing, planning and organizing, symptoms which are not confined to one named 'condition' (see Table 1.1). Children with dyslexia, DAMP and Asperger's syndrome may all have such movement learning difficulties as well as those with dyspraxia.

## Strategies to help

When parents share their worries about their children being slow to walk and talk, they often ask, 'What can we do?' One helpful strategy is to make regular observations of exactly when their children did what they did and to record them in the form of a diary. Dated observations provide firm evidence of progress to share with a professional should this prove necessary. Some useful observations might concern the children's motor milestones, e.g.:

1   for babies: holding the head up; sitting without support; rolling over; crawling; standing with support then unaided; reaching and grasping with increasing dexterity and, importantly, being able to let go; using the pincer grip to pick up objects;
2   for toddlers: walking; crawling; climbing stairs (noting whether a step together or a single passing foot action is used); scribbling with a pencil; coping with a spoon; drinking from a cup without too much mess; being able to say words clearly;
3   for 5-year-olds: drawing; early attempts at writing (note pencil control and pencil grip); using a knife and fork; coping with stairs and uneven surfaces; enjoying moving objects, e.g. swings, roundabouts;
4   for children of 8+ years: tying laces; being able to put clothes on in the right order; getting ready in time; riding a bike; catching a ball; joining in games; being able to do more than one thing at a time, e.g. running and kicking a ball, carrying a bag onto an escalator.

Activities which are avoided help to identify any movement patterns which are difficult, e.g. crawling, puzzles which need parts fitted together, climbing on a frame, other combined movements which need complex coordination.

### Actions at the midline of the body

A second strategy is to focus on any action which requires two hands to work together at the midline of the body, or crossing over the midline, e.g. fastening buttons or zips, opening a jar, winding a yo-yo. Some children develop avoidance strategies such as changing a pencil from one hand to the other to draw a circle.

A third is to check whether the child has a dominant hand/foot/ear/eye or if confused laterality is causing problems. One example of this would be the child attempting to score a goal and 'fumbling with his feet' because he cannot decide which foot to use for the shot. If this kind of confusion happens, the child may need support in making decisions through experimenting (to find which hand/ foot is most comfortable to use and which gives the best results) and being helped to make decisions about which to use. Teachers can 'test' laterality by placing an object just out of the child's reach and watching the child pick it up. The object has to be placed equidistantly from each hand or foot and the 'test' needs to be repeated several times before any definite conclusion is drawn. Children may need time and a calm atmosphere to enable them to decide which is the most comfortable and successful way for them. Observations of movements which still cause problems should lead to teachers simplifying the actions and/or reducing the contextual demands, then gradually building them up again so that the more complex pattern is proficient.

## Analyzing movement patterns

Once the observation that children are having difficulty moving well has been made, the next plan must be to analyze their movement patterns to try to discover the point(s) of breakdown.

The first thing is to recognize that there are four components within movement which need to be observed to find exactly where any difficulty lies, i.e.:

1   Conceptualizing the idea: can the children explain what they have or wish to do?
2   Planning and organizing: can the children organize themselves and any resources to allow the movement to happen?
3   Movement abilities: have the children the movement abilities (e.g. the balance, coordination, strength and speed) to allow them to carry out the movement?
4   Short-term memory: do the children remember how to do the movements from previous tries and can they use feedback to help them?

Answering these four questions helps to clarify the exact nature of the difficulty. If they are not considered, the wrong kind of support could be given.

What competencies are needed?

1   Conceptualizing the idea, e.g. imagination; previous experience; a role model; confidence in one's own ability; recognition and selection of possibilities.
2   Planning, organizing and sequencing, e.g. thinking ahead; ordering actions; anticipating obstacles, problem-solving (e.g. how to cross a gap or score a goal or knowing how to plan to meet a target); making decisions about the different possibilities of solving challenges. Devising, remembering and keeping rules are also important. Getting the body ready before, during and after movements, i.e. knowing which body parts to move at what time; knowing how to move sequentially; collecting and organizing the necessary resources at the correct time.
3   Movement abilities, e.g. being able to move in a coordinated, balanced and rhythmical way, i.e. using the correct selection of strength, speed and space; being able to adjust movements to suit a new environment.
4   Memorizing abilities, e.g. being able to repeat previously learned movements; being able to use the feedback from one try to improve the next; habituating movements so that they become automatic.

How can parents and teachers best help any movement difficulty? They have to be sure that their support covers all four aspects of movement. One interaction might help to explain this.

The child has chosen to walk along a bench stepping over beanbags.

Planning advice before the action:

Teacher:   What are you going to do? (to confirm that the child has planned the action).

Child:   I am going to balance along the bench stepping over lots of beanbags, then jump down at the end and then run back to you again (checking that the child has a mental picture of the sequence).

Teacher:   Right, good idea – now get everything ready (checking if the child can organize the resources, e.g. asking for help to place the bench away from other 'traffic' or collecting an appropriate number of beanbags from a basket or cupboard and placing them step-width apart on the bench; the child has to visualize a series of organizations, then carry them out).

Teacher:   Are you ready? Now, show me which foot will step onto the bench first? Several tries of stepping on without going onto the full sequence could be needed to establish the dominant foot and the distance the body should be from the bench for the best push up.

Child:   I'll push up with my right foot and pull the other one up beside it – and I'll keep it up high so that it doesn't knock into the beanbag! (child describes the movement to reveal the action plan).

Teacher:   Let's try that. Now tell me, where do you need to be very strong?

Child:  Pushing up onto the bench and then when I jump down to land I need to hold on with my tummy muscles so that I don't fall over.

Teacher: Remember to wait and steady yourself and feel balanced after you step over each beanbag – don't be in a hurry … ready?

Then, helpful 'movement advice' during the action might be:

Teacher:   Remember to push the top of your head up high. Just glance at the beanbag, step over and get your balance before moving on. Take it slowly. Can you use your arms to help you balance? Show me where they are. Pause before you jump down. Can you remember to bend your knees and spring up again before you run round back to the start?

These kinds of comments which remind the children to think about where each body part functions in space might seem too basic for many children. Those who have movement learning difficulties, however, very often need to slow down and think about how their bodies are going to respond to the task that has been set. They need to think about the position of their bodies as they move so that their body awareness is developed. Gradually as simple sequences are internalized – and only if they are done well are they useful building blocks for more difficult challenges – then the pace of the action can be speeded up so that the natural momentum of the sequence takes over and provides the flow which helps movement to be efficient.

It can be seen that moving well is a complex task. As the actual patterns are carried out, the children are making decisions about the type of movement they wish to do, the strength and speed they need, the space they require and if they will be safe.

## Movement abilities

### Balance

In Chapter 3, the importance of the vestibular sense in promoting balance was emphasized and indeed this competence is the key to moving well. It was also stressed that the vestibular sense worked with all the other senses and that any deficit could impair other forms of sensory acuity. So helping children balance in a movement lesson can have lots of benefits, even helping the other aspects of sensory development.

Balance is necessary in both movement (dynamic balance) and stillness (static balance). Some authors call balance, 'postural control'. This does suggest the wider application of the ability to balance and shows that it is not just the ability to stand on one leg without toppling over. Balance sustains the position of the body in the air in a jump; it steadies the body in a throwing action; it helps control in turning corners or running down stairs. So if adults suspect that any child has a poor sense of balance, observations should be made when the child is moving and when the child tries to be still.

### Coordination

Coordination is the ability to control the independent body parts involved in an action and make them work together efficiently to achieve some goal. Different tasks need the body parts to be sequenced in different ways and so there are different kinds of coordination, e.g. hand–eye coordination needed in catching a ball or threading a needle, hand–foot coordination as in kicking skills or jumping up to reach a target. There is whole body coordination used when more advanced sports skills such as skiing are tackled. These are different competencies and it shouldn't be assumed that because children can manage one, that they can achieve the others. When coordination is problematic, simplifying the requirements can help, e.g. having children sit as they do their drawings rather than standing at an easel can reduce the balance requirements and let them concentrate on their hand–eye coordination. Similarly, building up batting skills through small cooperative chal-lenges, e.g. 'Who can get a rally of five hits with a partner?' can instill the basic skills giving the children the chance to practise before larger competitive games.

### Rhythm

Rhythmic movement is efficient movement because one part of the movement flows into the next with no waste of energy. The momentum from one part of the movement carries over to the next and providing the correct amount of strength and speed has been used and the transitions have been coped with the movement is fluid and easy on the mover and on the eye of the observer.

Sometimes helping the children to appreciate the intrinsic rhythm of a phrase of movement can help their movement. Listening to the sound of a shuttlecock as it hits the cork bat and contrasting the sound when 'success' and 'disaster' happen is one example. This sound can be helpful because it tells whether more or less strength is required to prevent the rally breaking down. Counting out the rhythm in activities like learning to skip can be helpful too.

### Timing movements

Children with movement learning difficulties are often slow in reacting to a stimulus, e.g. 'Go', and in an effort to catch up, their subsequent movement patterns can be rushed and ineffective. They can be helped by being given advance warning of what is going to happen – perhaps by the teacher fixing eye contact with them and asking, 'Are you ready?' so that concentration can be at its peak before 'Go' explodes.

But if children find lots of movements difficult, if they are clumsy and awkward or lack confidence in trying to move on the ground far less on large apparatus, what can be done?

### Perceptual–motor programmes

Many primary/junior schools have now established short (15–20 minutes) daily inputs of planned activities called perceptual–motor programmes (the name perceptual included in recognition of the part played by the sensory integration that tells us where, when and how to move. All the teachers who have participated have recognized the difference in their children. They have reported that their children have shown greater confidence and willingness to stay with a task. They have also been more settled afterwards in class because the activity has given them enough sensory stimulation to hold them for a while; in general terms, 'they have been more in control of themselves and their belongings'.

In many programmes, children with recognized 'labels', e.g. dyslexia, dyspraxia, ADHD or Asperger's syndrome, work alongside children who have none but who perhaps lack confidence in their own abilities and would benefit from such a programme. Others, who perhaps use too much strength and speed and so need to know how to approach tasks calmly and carefully so that the end result is pleasing, can join in too. Finely built children are another group who may avoid movement, afraid to get hurt in the rough and tumble of noisy games. Their confidence can be built up by participating in non-contact activities which are not too challenging and where staff offer support. So there are lots of reasons why children join a perceptual–motor programme and 'once the programme is underway, other children usually want to take part' (school physical education teacher). The programmes are popular with the children too, maybe not always for the right reasons. 'I'll get on that programme next term', said 7-year-old Sean, 'for it looks a lot better than boring old maths!'

Case study 17

Listen to Gaynor and Bill, parents of Simon and Fay, 11-year- old twins who have dyslexia, dyspraxia and some hints of Asperger's syndrome shown in their reluctance to communicate with others. They are both of average general ability with good vocabularies. They explained,

> When the school said to us that they would like the twins to become involved in a perceptual movement programme, we were a bit uneasy. They already spent quite a bit of time at learning support for their spelling and reading although they are both good at maths. We didn't really want them to be out of the 'normal' classroom for any more time because we thought they would be missing things like science and environmental studies and subjects like that. However, the school arranged for administration time to be used and the children were asked if they could go in to school 10 minutes early. That was time they usually hung around anyway, so that was a good solution.
>
> We knew that 'doing things' was a problem, particularly for Simon. Despite being bright, he still can't tie laces or open jars or fasten the straps on his schoolbag. Velcro has kept us sane! Although we thought the programme might help, we didn't know how he would cope with taking off his outdoor clothes which had just taken him hours to put on. Fay is better at these sorts of things; her fine motor skills are better developed, possibly because she's always enjoyed drawing and painting, but she doesn't like sports at all. She is a timid girl, very afraid of getting hurt and maybe because of this not very good at making friends. Of course they always have each other for company and they seem content.

Bill then explained what had convinced them to allow the twins to take part. He said,

> The parents of the first group of children who had already tried the programme had a meeting one evening and invited new parents to come along. The staff took us down to the hall and explained what would be going on. It turned out that there wouldn't be any rushing around – it was careful walking along benches and aiming beanbags into hoops, crawling over obstacles and learning to skip – that sort of thing, so we decided to let the children take part for the first term at least. They both liked the teachers who would be in charge of the programme and they knew that some of the more confident children from their class were

going to be there too. The main thing was the school put it over that they had been chosen to take part – and because there were very bright children in the group, our two believed that was true, so the whole thing got off to a good start. The children had lots of fun, they recognized that their movements were getting better and the class teacher said that the improvement in their confidence had been 'phenomenal'.

## Safety – the most important thing of all

Above all else the children must be safe, so checks must constantly be made to ensure that they won't be hurt. It can be a good idea to have one member of staff responsible for different 'duties', e.g. checking the safety of the large apparatus – so that in the bustle of coping with a group of children moving all over the place, this doesn't get overlooked.

Some checks before the programme begins:

- Has each child been cleared to take part? Have medical conditions been identi-fied against the level of activity which could be undertaken – remembering that some children may attempt too much?
- Can safety checks – on cards – be positioned on walls and equipment as reminders for children with poor short-term memories? Visual aids help, e.g. 'Only three children on the climbing frame at once'. Picture cards may be required for poor readers or for those who do not understand number concepts.
- Have the children suitable footwear that will not slip? Are the soles of their trainers flexible enough to prevent slipping on climbing apparatus?
- Is the apparatus spaced out far enough to prevent bumping?
- Are the mats thick enough to protect children who fall heavily?
- Is the apparatus stable and securely fixed?
- In case of an accident, do all the staff (including temporary members, students and/or parent helpers) understand the safety procedures to be followed?

And so programmes should not be undertaken lightly. Safety is always para-mount – visualizing what children 'just might' be tempted to do is essential as there is always one child who can 'do the unexpected and fall' if planners haven't considered every possibility!

## What could the content of the programme be?

Three important reminders before such programmes are compiled:

1 Strengthening exercises need some resistance to make the muscles work harder.
2 Mobilizing exercises need the limbs to move through the whole of their range.
3 If there is any unexplained or unforeseen rigidity or pain, the help of a GP and/ or physiotherapist has to be sought. No exercise should cause stress or pain.

Although the different children in the programme will have very specific needs which must be catered for, the programme can have lots of variety. The emphasis should be on doing movements well, i.e. with control and poise.

There will be activities to develop,

- Gross motor skills, i.e. movements which involve the large muscle groups working together, coordinated to produce actions – often called the basic movement patterns – such as crawling, walking, running, jumping, hopping and skipping. These can be done making patterns on the floor, on low apparatus, in twos – perhaps in a meeting and parting sequence or building floor patterns together. The children enjoy an accompaniment of percussion or music which also helps their rhythmical appreciation – there are lots of ways to add interest.
- Games skills patterns. Usually gross movements with the added challenge of apparatus such as throwing and catching, aiming, kicking, passing and receiving, dodging and marking, striking or hitting (as in racquet sports) are popular. These can be done individually, e.g. 'beating my own score' types of games, or with a partner, then possibly building the small game into a mini competition just to make the activities seem like real games.
- Fine motor skills, i.e. movements which use the small muscle groups, often to produce intricate results, such as speaking clearly, colouring in, tying laces, playing a musical instrument, fastening buttons, carrying and placing objects securely.

NB Many of these happen at the midline of the body and involve the two hands doing different things at the same time. These can be impossible for some children so these tasks have to be carefully monitored. Children may be able to carry out an action satisfactorily as a closed skill, e.g. catching a ball which has been sympathetically thrown to them, however, they are likely to be totally lost when the environment changes, e.g. when the same skill has to be adjusted to meet the demands of a game, i.e. an open skill. Practice to achieve competence in the first needs to be followed by changing the equipment, e.g. to a smaller, harder ball. Gradually making the environment less stable, perhaps by having other children running past so that attention could be diverted and the child has to concentrate to keep on track, would be the next step. These are all necessary before a child with movement difficulties can make the leap from single skills practices to playing in a game. And so challenge can be added by changing the environmental demands rather than changing the skill pattern itself.

Sometimes staff are reluctant to begin programmes because they are unsure of ideas and doubt their ability to keep a programme going. There are many books full of suggestions and many classroom rhymes can be acted out in the hall giving a much better chance to develop awareness of space. Many old fashioned singing games, e.g. 'In and out the dusty bluebells' where the children have to pass under arches made by the group, hold just the kinds of movement challenges children with movement learning difficulties need. And so learning to move need not involve equipment or apparatus at all. Lots of fun and competence can be gained through the expressive side of moving – through dance or drama – and this can be a very enjoyable introduction to movement and save teachers worrying about children being hurt. Using action words to build drama or dance sequences can be very satisfying and these can link with imaginative writing and/or oral storytelling. Phrases such as 'the lions prowled and pounced' or 'the fireworks exploded' or 'the aliens bounced on their springy legs' – or whatever the children decide aliens do – can be tried out. Percussion to accompany the movement helps keep the lesson lively and helps the awareness of rhythm.

Finally, all children have to learn to move safely in different environments so that they can cope with the activities of everyday living. Trying things out while experienced observers are there to watch and support is surely the very best thing that they can do.

## Some activities to help body awareness, coordination, balance and control

All sorts of rhymes and jingles name body parts, e.g. Head, shoulders, knees and toes, Under the spreading chestnut tree, Simon Says.

NB Make sure the game involves the backs of the heels and backs of shoulders as children who have poor body awareness are likely to have difficulty knowing where their backs are. They can be confused by instructions asking them to 'stand with your back near the wall', they can find passing belts around their backs difficult and wiping at the toilet impossible. Lots of body awareness games help, e.g.:

Tap-time
Tap on your shoulder and tap on your nose,
Clasp hands together then do you suppose
You could tap on two elbows, then tap on two knees
Then tap, oh so gently, wherever you please?

Stand very still now, and push your head tall
Stretch to the ceiling, be sure you don't fall,
Curl up in a tiny ball, let's hear you count to ten
1, 2, 3, 4, 5, 6, 7, 8, 9, 10!
Hold quite still, then jump right up
And then begin again.

Lots of jingles like the one above, but with piano and guitar accompaniment, are in *Jingle Time* by Christine Macintyre, with music for piano and percussion by Mike Carter. Published by David Fulton Publisher, 414 Chiswick High Street, London W4 5TF.

### Progressions

Using two hands to do different actions can be tricky but children enjoy them if they are given time to think. Some children will become flustered if speed is necessary. Rather, give them time to feel the parts mentioned and be sure of where they are in relation to one another.

'Put one hand on your knee and the other one on the back of your head. Change them over.' The children can take it in turns to suggest places. Once this is established, then choosing parts which involve crossing the midline of the body can highlight difficulties such as confused laterality or poor hand dominance. 'Put one hand on the other knee' (teacher can demonstrate the crossing over).

For older ones:

> Show me your right hand,
> Wave it very high
> Stretch it and stretch it
> Right up to the sky!
> Now stretch up your left hand,
> Make it just as tall
> Fix your hands above your head and
> Twirl and twirl ... and fall!

### Concentrating on shapes

Aerial drawing of letters – one child draws a letter and another guesses what it was. 'Make the letter bigger and bigger till you have to jump off the ground to reach up and crouch down to do the bottom part.'

### Progression

While sitting leaning back on hands, draw the letter with you toes: use the right foot then the left one. Stretch one foot up high, wiggle it and place it gently beside the other (good for abdominal and leg strengthening, control and balance). Repeat with the other. Try two feet together. Lie down. Lift feet 12 cm from the ground. Hold them steady for a count of six. Then lower them gently (partner helps judge the distance feet are from the ground).

### Prone kneeling position (crawling position)

All sorts of crawling activities are essential for improving coordination:

- through a tunnel
- along a bench
- through a tunnel then climb onto a low box and jump off.

Building crawling into a sequence of actions lets an assessor see whether it is the planning aspect of movement which is difficult or remembering instructions, or whether it is the actual movement, perhaps moving from the crawling position to the climbing one, which is most problematic. This narrows the focus for support.

## Leg strengthening

In the swimming pool, walking through waist deep water taking big strides. Standing comfortably on a mat, lowering to sit and standing again slowly, with control. Children who find this difficult can try in twos facing one another, holding hands to lower themselves gently onto a mat. Sitting they can see-saw back and forward before they pull up to standing again.

Any jumping activity – over ropes placed loosely over skittles, jumping to score a basket, jumping two feet together to cover distance (very difficult). Varying the distance between skittles, e.g. putting them closer together or further apart, or changing the layout so that the children have to change direction can let observers see whether the children can cope by altering their movement patterns to suit the changes.

## Hand dominance/confused laterality

Picking up beanbag, passing it overhead to change hands; passing it round the body (children call out 'change' when the beanbag passes from one hand to the next).

In a circle, passing the beanbag round like 'Pass the Parcel' (receive in one hand, pass it to the other and stretch out to the side to pass it on). This develops a sense of laterality or sidedness. Repeat with a ball which is harder to grasp.

Repeat with a heavy cylinder (a tube shaped crisp carton filled with sand is ideal).

## Walking and running

Walking forwards heel to toe for 5 metres. (Note any extraneous arm curling.)

Walk for 5 metres, run for 10 metres and walk for the last 5. Where to change the action can be clearly marked out by beanbags placed on the floor. (Observers should note control and anticipation of the change. Do the children adapt their speed? Do they lumber rather than appear agile? Do they get to the point of change and then try to adjust their stride rather than anticipating it?)

The game 'Wire and Wall' is a very good way to assess planning and control. Two children begin together covering the same distance but on a different path. One runs to the far wall, comes back to the starting position then runs to 'the wire', a mark on the floor halfway to the wall and back. The other child runs to the wire and back, then to the wall and back.

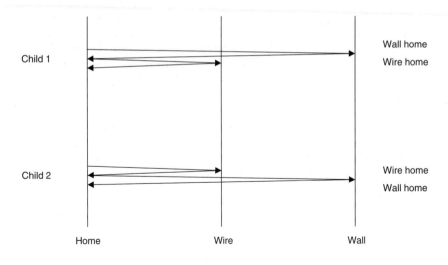

*Figure 5.1* Wire and wall

Can each child remember his own pathway? Can they change direction without falling over? When the game changes so that each child takes his partner's route, can he still remember where to run? (see Figure 5.1).

A video showing a programme in action with comments from the head teacher, the support for learning teacher, the class teacher, a parent of a child on the 'Perceptual–motor programme' and, most importantly, the child himself, can be obtained from MALTS, Edinburgh University, Holyrood Road, Edinburgh EH 8 8AQ (£25).

## Movement and health

If children consider they are not good at movement activities they are likely to avoid exercise.

There can be health costs, especially if snacks are taken instead.

## Building health, strength and mobility

When children have enticing sedentary hobbies such as computing and play stations, the effects of not enough exercise can affect the children's health. Newspapers are full of stories of obesity in children, some even claiming that by age six 10 per cent of children are overweight. Gallahue (1993) is just one of the many researchers who have responded by listing the benefits of exercise. He claims that these are:

1   Increased strength and endurance, which
    •   stimulates bone growth

- increases bone mineralization
- reduces susceptibility to injury, and
- enhances body image
2. Improved levels of cardiovascular capacity, which
   - improves lung capacity
   - strengthens the heart muscle
   - improves circulation, and
   - aids stress reduction
3. Greater flexibility, which
   - helps prevent injury
   - increases work or play efficiency
   - improves motor performance
   - increases the range of actions, and
   - promotes fluidity of action.

This list shows why it is important that parents and teachers try to ensure that their children learn to enjoy movement activities. If they do their movement skills increase with the spin off benefits to personal, social and intellectual development too.

# Chapter 6

# Inclusive approaches for children with specific learning difficulties

'Inclusion' must be the 'buzz' word in education in the early years of the twenty-first century. The word is used constantly in national documents, academic journals and professional texts and is the topic which dominates many staff development days and continuing professional development courses. It has become apparent, however, that the word means different things to different people.

In some schools, inclusion is regarded as the placement of children considered to have special needs in a mainstream school. Inclusion is therefore deemed to be complete as soon as the children are placed in the school. Other schools consider that inclusion implies that all children should have 'full access' to an existing curriculum but that help will be required. An army of personnel may be recruited to support both the children and their teachers. Other schools appreciate that full access to a full curriculum is neither possible nor desirable and they set about changing their school, their curriculum and their aims and objectives to respond to the diversity of need within their school.

Booth (1998) defines inclusion as 'the process of increasing the participation of learners within and reducing their exclusion from, the cultures, curricula and communities of neighbourhood centres of learning'. It is written in response to claims that many children may have been marginalised within a class through being misunderstood. Sometimes this has led to them working in a solitary, non-inclusive manner.

What then are the key issues to be considered during this process with regard to children with specific learning difficulties?

## The curriculum

### An appropriate curriculum

Bernstein (2002) claims that a learning difficulty can appear whenever children 'hit a brick wall they cannot climb with their particular set of competencies'. She believes that a learning difficulty is a failure to adapt to the learning environment. Since it is not possible for every child to achieve what have traditionally been considered appropriate competencies no matter how much support is available, the school needs to consider what changes require to be made to both the curriculum and the learning environment to offer children successful learning experiences. The learning tasks can be matched to the learning needs rather than to pre-existing expectations. This means that the curriculum becomes a flexible, responsive vehicle, which helps children to reach their maximum potential. This may appear to be an unattainable goal but if schools can respond by offering such flexibility and by working towards an ethos where diversity is appreciated, then the process of inclusion can begin.

The phrase 'barriers to learning' has been used in the past. Today these barriers are recognized as existing within the school rather than within the child. By undertaking an audit of the curriculum on offer, schools can identify where change is necessary. This is one of the first steps in the inclusion process.

## Differentiation

### In the curriculum

Schools which offer the most successful learning experiences are likely to be those which have carefully considered the question of differentiation and regard it as something more complex than 'simplifying the worksheet'. 'Differentiation is the attitude, approach and structure that makes flexibility possible' (SCCC 1993). Both the pace of presenting the input and the level of the content can be adapted to suit the needs of particular children. On the other hand differentiation by outcome, i.e. what is asked for, in terms of amount of work to be done, as well as the level of work means that many more children can be successful. They can complete their work and be seen to cope alongside their peers. It is important that each outcome is seen as being equally valued by the teacher. In this way all the children can have pleasure in their success.

### In the teaching approach

Meeting the needs of children with specific learning difficulties often means reconsidering the teaching approach. There is a temptation for teachers to teach in the way they themselves learn. This may not suit the learning styles of children with specific learning difficulties. To be effective the teachers must decentre, i.e. understand the preferred way of learning of their individual pupils and change their teaching to match. This is not easy but very necessary if the children's learning is to be eased.

## An individualized curriculum

### Accommodations

An important strategy in the support of pupils with specific learning difficulties is the consideration of accommodations. These are not the same as differentiation.

When teachers differentiate work they consider the input, processing and output of information by each child. When contemplating accommodations, teachers consider whether it is absolutely necessary for children to 'conform' to the usual arrangements that may add to their difficulties. As an example, Harry, in case study 12, was given an accommodation by his teacher. She appreciated that his tactile difficulties caused him to dislike close contact with other children and reckoned that he would pay more attention if he was allowed to stay in his seat rather than join the group on the carpet.

### Examples of accommodations

Children with memory and sequencing difficulties who have made an attempt to learn multiplication tables can be given an accommodation in the form of a calculator or 144 square. Some may claim that the memory is unlikely to improve if not encouraged by learning multiplication tables, but what often happens is that children suffer many tears and frustrations before the answers are eventually committed to memory. However, if, in order to give the answer to a multiplication fact, the children can only begin at the start of the table and work through to the required number, this is a slow, possibly inaccurate method. The use of a calculator is clearly quicker and less of an ordeal for the children who can then participate with their peer group.

Some children with specific learning difficulties have great difficulty copying from the board. They may have a poor memory or they may experience difficulty holding the information in their visual memory as the eyes move from looking at the board (vertically placed) to the book (horizontally placed). This is seldom a case of 'practice makes perfect' and much frustration can be avoided if a photocopy is placed on the children's desks.

Children considered to have ADHD are sometimes asked to sit immediately in front of the teacher when the class/group is gathered around to go over a particular topic. The 'theory' is that the teacher can 'keep an eye' on the child, hopefully preventing any unnecessary, excess movement. This approach is based on the assumption that the child can control the hyperactivity and is more likely to do so under the teacher's eye. In practice, of course, the child cannot do this and is even less likely to do so sandwiched between the teacher and the rest of the class. An accommodation in this case would be to allow the child to sit at the edge of the group and to move if the urge is felt. In this way the child can move away from the group causing less of a disturbance.

Accommodations are offered to circumvent difficulties. However, in order to support such approaches the ethos of the class needs to be one where difference is acknowledged, discussed and supported. All children in the class need to know that they, in their turn, will be offered any necessary accommodations.

## Individualized educational plans

IEPs can be critically useful documents when aims and targets are agreed and understood by school personnel, parents and the children themselves. In this way the children are part of the planning process; they understand the shared aims and are therefore more likely to try to achieve them. However, recent research reported by the Scottish Executive (2002), has revealed that minimal consultation with either parents or children is the norm and that little evidence of plans being evaluated has been able to be gathered. There is a danger, therefore, of IEPs becoming a time-consuming paper exercise containing narrow, limiting, but easily measurable targets.

An IEP should be integrated into the planning process and not regarded as an 'add on' for a particular child. It is a way of sharing information and understanding children's strengths and difficulties. Agreed aims and targets should be shared so that the document becomes a whole school response to children's learning.

Individualization of aspects of the curriculum is sometimes necessary for children with a specific learning difficulty. The danger here is that 'individualized' can become 'individual' with the children at risk of being offered special programmes which involve them in solitary work. If some children need a specialized programme rather than or as well as the aforementioned strategies which happen in the classroom, it is important that such interventions are regarded as 'part of the norm' rather than perceived as something 'different'.

## Inclusive approaches

### Ethos

No matter how early children's specific learning difficulties are recognized or how appropriate any support may be, children who have specific difficulties are unlikely to succeed unless their 'difference' is recognized and appreciated by the whole school. Many schools and parents worry that appropriate resources may not be available but the way forward is not in an array of resources, programmes or an extra computer. The way forward is for all teachers to understand the implications for children with specific learning difficulties and to teach with empathy and understanding. This can be fostered through continuing professional development.

### Continuing professional development

Continuing professional development opportunities can help to raise awareness of specific learning difficulties. It is neither practical nor necessary for every teacher to become an 'expert' but each teacher must be able to recognize the indicators and implications for learning, and know how to prepare appropriate support strategies. It is also necessary that teachers know where to turn for further advice and support. This is offered through policies and guidelines.

## Policies and guidelines

Guidelines are necessary to inform teachers and parents of ways in which the school will set about identifying specific learning difficulties, how they will assess and support their children and how the chosen support strategies and interventions will be evaluated.

Careful consideration is necessary as to the form and content of such documents. Many schools now have policies addressing children with dyslexia. Do these schools also require policies covering dyspraxia, ADHD, and SLI or should the policy address all specific learning difficulties as one? Is a separate policy necessary to cover every eventuality or is one policy addressing effective teaching and learning the answer? Given the overlap or co-occurrence of difficulties one comprehensive document could suffice.

Whatever form a school selects, it is important that the guidelines are a practical working document, drawn up by members of the support staff after consultation with the whole staff. It is also essential that they are reviewed and revised as necessary. Policies and guidelines should recognize the importance of time for liaison.

## Time for liaison

A network of support built around pupils and teachers can reassure and facilitate learning. The class teacher is often expected to be the expert in all areas of learning but support in the form of consultancy or cooperative teaching is helpful. Some class teachers benefit from the support of a SENCO, school-based or visiting learning support teacher, or other visiting professional. Too often, however, visiting professionals are not timetabled to liaise with the class teacher, therefore there is little opportunity for discussing the pupils' progress. The management team can facilitate consultancy and collaboration between class teacher and other personnel involved in support. Joint planning and evaluation with another professional can be a useful support for a class teacher. Sometimes this kind of cooperation can avoid the need for more intrusive intervention. Liaison time is also needed between class teacher and support assistants.

## Support assistants

Classroom support is a welcome feature of today's classroom but class teachers must know how to manage this support. Support assistants who work with children who have specific learning difficulties can often be most effective if used for particular tasks, for example reading or scribing for the children. They may also reinforce programmes undertaken by speech and language therapists or occupational therapists. Managing any ICT by perhaps scanning and incorporating text into software programs is another example of appropriate use of support assistants.

This type of focussed support is more beneficial than an assistant sitting beside children most of the day offering general help. This can act as a barrier to the children interacting with their peer group. Children need their own time and space and opportunities to chat with others. The use of support assistants should therefore be carefully considered. The dangers of 'learned helplessness' must also be appreciated, i.e. children letting their assistant do things they could manage for themselves.

Parents sometimes become anxious if a support assistant who they regard as primarily in the class to support their child is not constantly at the child's side. Such a situation requires parent/teacher communication.

### Parent/teacher communication

Parents and teachers together can agree on the frequency and type of support offered. It is also important that parents explain to the teacher if their child has to do a regular programme of exercises or perhaps go swimming to help develop movement skills. These are fundamental in giving confidence and competence and time should be given for this. The teacher may be willing to dispense with homework and allow these activities to stand in their stead. There is little use expecting children with poor shoulder and arm control to write well. It is much better for them to have the strengthening work that will facilitate writing with pleasure when their fine motor skills have been improved.

It is understandable that parents want to support their children's learning at home. To make this work, good communication between home and school is essential. It is unlikely that children who have spent a great deal of time on spelling in school will be motivated to spend more at home unless the content and the approach have been carefully considered. Some interesting and stimulating ways of consolidating work covered in class can be offered at home if home and school are jointly planning and evaluating.

One rewarding way parents can support at home is by giving children opportunities to do things they enjoy. Many children have particular talents and/or interests in areas which can be encouraged by parents. Time spent attending a drama group, participating in sport, learning a musical instrument or following any particular interest or strength is time well spent when opportunities to succeed abound.

## Conclusion

Teachers' own continuing professional development offers opportunities to learn about the nature of the specific learning difficulties that children in their classes are likely to display. Teachers are the first point of contact, therefore they must be familiar with the relevant indicators. However, teachers need to know that they are not alone and are not required to formally assess their children. They need to know that expertise is available in the form of consultancy or collaborative teaching.

The aim of this book has been to encourage teachers to consider the whole child when a difficulty is identified rather than to attempt to match the child to any pre-existing set of indicators. There is no one test which will confirm any specific learning difficulty. Rather a set of observations and 'inner child' analyses is the first step and there is no one more appropriately placed or suitably qualified than the class teacher to undertake this investigation. This can then be supplemented by a more formal assessment which may be carried out by a suitably qualified member of the school staff or by another professional. Everyone who is involved, however, must look beyond the label to ensure that the whole child is assessed and appropriately supported in an inclusive setting.

# Appendix

## Definitions and/or diagnostic criteria for specific learning difficulties referred to in this book

### Attention deficit disorder (ADD)

This specific learning difficulty is characterized by serious and persistent difficulties with attention and impulse control. Children with ADD have severe difficulty focussing their attention, which quickly shifts from one activity to another. They are easily distracted and find it difficult to be still. If unidentified, educational progress is highly likely to be affected, as is the self-esteem.

In order to offer successful learning experiences teachers must have a good awareness of ADD, an appreciation of children's difficulties, a willingness to make changes in teaching style and allow accommodations in the classroom.

If hyperactivity is also present, the term Attention Deficit Hyperactivity Disorder (ADHD) is used (see below).

### Attention Deficit Hyperactivity Disorder (ADHD)

#### Diagnostic criteria

The onset of the problem must be before age seven, and the disturbance must last at least six months, during which at least eight of the following are present:

- Often fidgets with hands or feet or squirms in seat (in adolescents, this may be limited to subjective feelings of restlessness)
- Has difficulty remaining seated when required to do so
- Is easily distracted by extraneous stimuli
- Has difficulty awaiting turn in game or group situations
- Often blurts out answers to questions before they have been completed
- Has difficulty following through on instructions from others (not due to oppositional behaviour or failure of comprehension), for example, fails to finish chores

- Has difficulty sustaining attention in tasks or play activities
- Often shifts from one uncompleted activity to another
- Has difficulty playing quietly
- Often talks excessively
- Often interrupts or intrudes on others, for example, butts into other children's games
- Often does not seem to listen to what is being said to him or her
- Often loses things necessary for tasks or activities at school or at home (e.g. toys, pencils, books, assignments)
- Often engages in physically dangerous activities without considering possible consequences (not for purpose of thrill-seeking), for example, runs into street without looking.

Source: *Diagnostic and Statistical Manual for Mental Disorders* (third edn rev.), 1987. Washington, DC: American Psychiatric Association, pp. 53–4. Copyright © 1987 by the American Psychiatric Association.

This disorder is usually spotted quickly through observations because the children's inability to be still severely disrupts themselves and others. They find it extraordinarily difficult to pay attention, to cut out distractors and concentrate, and other people can quickly become impatient. Their peers may well retaliate if their games or their work is spoiled. Children with ADHD are impulsive and may rush into actions without considering the consequences. In school extra help may be required to ensure that the children are safe.

### Asperger's syndrome

Asperger's syndrome is a form of autism, but children with Asperger's syndrome do not usually have the accompanying learning difficulties experienced by those with autism.

Children with Asperger's syndrome typically have social difficulties. Many wish social contact and seek it out but find they cannot respond in an appropriate way. They find it difficult to express emotions or recognize them in others and because they do not predict what others know or are likely to do, their own responses are usually inappropriate. 'They may fit somewhere on the continuum of 'withdrawn to active, but odd' (Jordan and Powell 1995).

They do not have the additional intellectual difficulties found in children with autism but they have some rigidity of thought and behaviour. While they can tell their age, their name and some family details, e.g. if they have a brother or sister, interpreting how they themselves are progressing is difficult. This means they have a poorly formed self-esteem and need lots of evidence, e.g. in the form of stickers as rewards so that they have tangible enduring evidence that they are doing well.

The children's language skills may be well developed, indeed this is often an area of strength; however, despite verbal fluency, the skills of interaction are poorly understood. So the children switch topics, interrupt inappropriately, go off at a tangent or dominate the conversation by lack of appreciation of turn-taking. This is because of a lack of empathy as to how others are reacting and responding.

Obsessional features are common especially at times of stress. These can be more complex than in children described as autistic. Stereotyped actions and self-stimulatory episodes tend to occur if the children's sensory perception is flawed.

Children with Asperger's are likely to be described as awkward or clumsy because they find problems with coordination, which affects both their fine and gross motor skills. They are likely to have achieved their motor milestones late and so share this difficulty with children with dyspraxia and some with dyslexia.

### DAMP (deficit in attention, motor control and perception)

This term is used more in Scandinavian countries than in Britain. Many of the difficulties are those of dyspraxia, developmental coordination disorder and ADHD. As is the case in these other conditions too, children find difficulty in paying attention and staying still for the necessary length of time and this detracts from their ability to learn. They do attract attention but this can be to restrain them from danger because they may be impulsive, or to stop them distracting other children from their work.

Their poor movement coordination means that motor milestones are likely to be delayed causing frustration and being left out of social activities because of 'inability to do' things which other children take for granted. Other children may call them stupid (negatively affecting their self-esteem).

### Dyslexia

Dyslexia is a difficulty with information processing. It is genetic and manifests itself in different ways with each child displaying an individual pattern of difficulties. Dyslexia was traditionally thought to affect only the acquisition of reading and spelling skills but it is now known to affect many areas of learning such as organisational and sequencing skills, concept of time, short-term memory, auditory and visual perception and spoken language. Since there is no one generally accepted definition and since each child presents with a differing set of difficulties identification was traditionally problematic and some education authorities were slow to consider their policies and practice, a situation which caused tension between parents and schools.

The advent of new technology such as MRI scans (magnetic resonance imaging) confirms that there are differences between the brain of a dyslexic and a non-dyslexic. These differences, which cause difficulties with language based activities, are also considered to be responsible for the creative abilities and talents which many children with dyslexia display.

## Dyspraxia

Although the term dyspraxia is most often used in education, the diagnostic and statistical manual (DSM-IV) of the American Psychiatric Association uses the term Developmental Coordination Disorder (DCD) and offers five criteria for diagnosis.

- There is a marked impairment in the development of motor coordination.
- The impairment significantly interferes with academic achievement or activities of daily living.
- The coordination difficulties are not due to a general medical condition, e.g. cerebral palsy, hemiplegia or muscular dystrophy.
- It is not a pervasive developmental disorder.
- If developmental delay is evident, the motor difficulties are in excess of those usually associated with it.

## A summary

Being unable to move effectively and efficiently in different environments impacts on all aspects of daily life. Children find that they are unable to kick a ball, ride a bike or control a pencil, in other words lots of things which they would love to do are denied them and the social connotations of not being able to join in means that friendships are scarce. This leads to frustration and poor self-esteem. Often the large muscle groups are affected so that the basic movement patterns, e.g. walking and running, are achieved just within the 'normal' time scale but their execution is poor. Sometimes the smaller muscle groups which affect fine motor skills cause difficulties and activities such as writing, being able to chew with the mouth closed and speaking clearly are impaired. Children can find it difficult to know what to do, this affects their planning. They may also lack/alternatively lack the movement abilities, e.g. balance and coordination, to carry out their plans.

Adults who can make more choices about their activities still find that everyday life is curtailed and opportunities for further education and/or employment are reduced. Without help maturation does not do enough to remove difficulties with cutting bread, opening a jar, changing a light bulb, coping with an escalator or carrying a case to name but a few problem areas. At work difficulties with organizing resources, e.g. collating photocopies, packing shelves, designing layouts all cause problems yet there is no 'intellectual' reason why this should be so.

Constantly feeling clumsy and uncoordinated can leave people very vulnerable so that they begin to believe they are less useful, even less valuable people. Intervention can help and the new policies on inclusion are there to provide help at any stage of education or in the workplace. People affected by dyspraxia have to know that it is their right to be helped.

## Specific language impairment (SLI)

The term Specific Language Impairment is used to describe a significant difficulty with the development of language where language skills are considerably delayed and there is:

- a discrepancy between verbal and non-verbal skills on standardized tests
- no obvious sign of neurological damage
- no significant hearing impairment

Some children seem to experience difficulty with expressive language only and would appear to have normal comprehension, whilst others experience a difficulty only with comprehension. A percentage of children have difficulty with both.

Expressive difficulties can range from lack of use of the past tense or lack of use of plurals to an extreme difficulty in forming words or organizing speech. Children with comprehension difficulties may produce fluent speech but may have difficulty processing speech.

# Glossary

* extra information in the appendix.

**ABD**   Atypical brain development – a biological basis for learning difficulties.

**ADD***   Difficulty in holding attention/concentrating.

**ADHD***   As above plus hyperactivity.

**Apraxia**   Poor motor planning (praxis).

**Articulation**   The production of language – vowels and consonants used appropriately and clearly by the active and passive articulators in the mouth (active: soft palate, lips and tongue; passive: hard palate, teeth).

**Asperger's syndrome***   Considered to be a form of autism, children with Asperger's syndrome have difficulty with communication and social skills but do not have difficulties with learning.

**Auditory sense**   Ability to hear clearly; to discriminate between sounds which are similar and different; to hold the sounds in the memory long enough to act upon them in some way.

**Autism**   A disorder affecting communication, socialization and imagination.

**Balance**   Static balance: the ability to hold the body steady. Dynamic balance: the ability to be controlled in movement.

**Bilateral integration**   The ability to coordinate two sides of the body (doing different things) to carry out a task, e.g. scoring a goal/basket.

**Body awareness**   Knowing, through feeling rather than seeing, where each body part is in relation to the others and to outside objects (also called body scheme).

**Cluttering**   Very quick speech resulting in mumbling.

**Co-occurence**   The overlap of symptoms amongst different conditions.

**Coordination**   The ability to move efficiently and effectively in different environments.

**DAMP***   Deficit in attention, motor control and perception (Scandinavian term).

**Development**   The changing patterns (physical, intellectual, emotional, social and motor) which occur sequentially in all children.

**Directionality**   The ability to move in different directions (forwards, backwards, diagonally and sideways).

**Distractibility**   Difficulty keeping on task. Attention span very short.

**Dominance**    The preferred side used in tasks such as writing, kicking, opening a jar, etc.

**Dysarthria**    A condition affecting speech production resulting in slurred speech due to weak or imprecise movement of the speech organs.

**Dyslexia\***    Difficulty with processing information, particularly affecting reading and spelling.

**Dyspraxia\***    Poor movement planning leading to poor coordination.

**Fine motor skills**    The patterns which depend on the dexterity of the small muscle groups, e.g. picking up and replacing an object, writing, computing, speaking, blinking, etc.

**Floppiness**    Poor muscle tone allowing too much laxity in the joints making control difficult.

**Gross motor skills**    Movements which require coordination of the large muscle groups, e.g. walking, crawling, jumping.

**Habituation**    The ability to recall and reuse items stored in the memory automatically, i.e. without detailed planning.

**IEP**    An individualized educational plan (IEP) is a planning document which outlines long- and short-term targets for children with special educational needs.

**Kinesthetic development**    Increasing spatial awareness helping efficient movement and directionality.

**Maturation**    The inbuilt changes that happen in development.

**Midline**    A strong sense of the midline of the body helps movements be balanced as it provides spatial cues (distance and direction). Crossing the midline can be extremely difficult for children with poor hand or foot dominance. Tasks at the midline of the body, e.g. opening a jar, fastening a coat, wiping at the toilet, are problematic for many children with specific learning difficulties.

**Perception**    The brain's ability to make sense of information coming from the environment, through the different senses, to the brain.

**Phonological awareness**    Ability to hear the separate sounds within words.

**Posture**    The alignment of body parts during movement and in stillness.

**Praxis**    The ability to move efficiently and effectively in different environments.

**Proprioception**    The sensory input from nerve endings in the muscles which pass information about movement – where and how it is occurring.

**Reflexes**    Involuntary movement in response to a stimulus and the concurrent physiological process.

**Reflex inhibition programme**    Individual programmes to inhibit primitive reflexes which are hindering the development of postural ones.

**Sensory integration**    The ability to select and coordinate the information (input) coming from the environment (through the receptors in the body to the brain) to produce efficient and effective output.

**SENCO**    Special Educational Needs Coordinator (England)

**Sequencing**    The ability to order steps and stages so that they flow together in the correct order.

**Skilled movement**    The correct selection of strength, speed and space to provide momentum with control resulting in effective output.

**SLI**    Specific language impairment. Children who display a deficit in language ability yet have age-appropriate scores on non-verbal tests, and with no clear sign of neurological damage or hearing impairment.

**Spatial orientation**    The ability to judge distances and directions so that the positioning of the body in relation to outside objects is secure.

**Tactile defensiveness**    An extreme reaction to being touched or having personal space 'invaded'.

**Tone**    Appropriate muscle strength for the task to be done: hyper – too much; hypo – too little.

**Verbal dyspraxia**    Speech is poorly organized to the extent that it may be incomprehensible. Articulation may have to be relearned through speech and language therapy so that intelligibility follows.

**Vestibular sense**    The sense which feeds positional information to the brain. Essential for balanced movement/stillness.

**Visual sense**    Recognizes people, objects, distances and depths; objects as distinct from their background; parts from a whole object; relationships between people and objects; stimulates hand–eye coordination; helps learning by providing visual memory.

# Bibliography

AFASIC Scotland (2000) Glossary Sheets. Dundee Scottish Executive.

Ausubel, D.P. (1963) *School Learning: An Introduction to Educational Psychology*. London: Holt, Reinhart and Winston.

Ayres, J.A. (1972) *Sensory Integration and Learning Disorders*. Los Angeles: Western Psychological Services.

Barkley, R.A. (1990) 'Attention deficit disorders: history definition and diagnosis', in M. Lewis and S.M. Miller (eds) *Handbook of Developmental Psychopathology*, pp. 65–76. New York: Plenum Press.

Barkley, R.A. (1995) *Taking Charge of ADHD. The Complete Authoritative Guide for Parents*. New York: Guilford Press.

Bee, H. (1998) *Lifespan Development* (second edn) Harlow: Longman.

Bee, H. (1999) *The Growing Child* (second edn) Harlow: Longman.

Berndt, T.J. and Keefe, K. (1995) 'Friends' influence on social adjustment – motivational analysis'. Paper presented at the Society for Research in Child Development, Indianapolis, March.

Bernstein, J.H. (2002) 'Assessing the developing child: a neurodevelopmental perspective'. Paper presented at the British Psychological Society Paediatric Neuropsychology Training Day, Guy's Hospital, London, September.

Booth, T. (1998) 'England: inclusion and exclusion in a competitive system', in T. Booth and M. Ainscow (eds) *From them to us: An international study of inclusion in education*. London: Routledge.

Buzan, T. (1993) *The Mind Map Book*. London: BBC Worldwide Publishing.

Caan, W. (1998) 'Foreword', in M. Portwood, *Developmental Dyspraxia, Identificaton and Intervention: A Manual for Parents and Professionals* (second edn). London: David Fulton Publishers.

Caspi, A. and Moffitt, T.E. (1991) 'Individual differences are accentuated during periods of social change', *Journal of Personality and Social Psychology*, 61: 157–68.

Chesson, R. (1990) *The Child With Motor/Learning Difficulties*. Aberdeen: Royal Aberdeen Children's Hospital.

Cohen, D. and Strayer, J. (1996) 'Empathy in conduct disordered and comparison youth development', *Psychology*, 32: 988–98.

Cooley, C. (1962) *Human Nature and the Social Order*. New York: Charles Scribner.

Croll, P. and Moses, D. (1985) *One in Five*. London: Routledge and Kegan Paul.

Farnham-Diggory, S. (1992) *The Learning Disabled Child*. Cambridge, MA: Harvard University Press.

Fawcett, A.J. and Nicolson, R.I. (1995) 'Persistent deficits in motor skills of children with dyslexia', *Journal of Motor Behaviour*, 27: 235–40.

Gallahue, D. (1993) *Developmental Physical Education for Today's Children*. Dubuque: Brown Communications.

Gardner, H. (1983) *Frames of Mind. The Theory of Multiple Intelligence*. New York: Basic Books.

Goddard, S. (1996) *A Teacher's Window into the Child's Mind*. Eugene, OR: Fern Ridge Press.

Griffiths, M. (2002) *Study Skills and Dyslexia in the Secondary School*. London: David Fulton Publishers.

Harter, S. (1990) 'Processes underlying adolescent self-concept formulation', in R. Montemayor, G.R. Adams and P. Gullota (eds) *From Childhood to Adolescence. A transitional period?* Newbury Park, CA: Sage.

Howe, M.J.A. (1989) 'Separate skills or general intelligence: the autonomy of human abilities', *British Journal of Educational Psychology*, 59: 351–60.

Jordan, R. and Powell, S. (1995) *Understanding and Teaching Children with Autism*. Chichester: John Wiley.

Kaplan, B., Dewey, D.M., Crawford, S.G. and Wilson, B.N. (2001) 'The term comorbidity is of questionable value in reference to developmental disorders: data and theory', *Journal of Learning Disabilities*, 34(6) Nov/Dec.

Keen, D. (2001) 'Specific neurodevelopmental disorders'. Paper presented at the Conference on the Needs of Children with Specific Developmental Difficulties, Bishop Auckland, February.

Kirby, A. (1999) *The Hidden Handicap*. London: Souvenir Books.

Levine, M. (1994) *Educational Care*. Cambridge, MA: Educators Publishing Service Inc.

Macintyre, C. (2001) *Dyspraxia 5–11*. London: David Fulton Publishers.

Macintyre, C. (2002) *Play for Children with Special Educational Needs*. London: David Fulton Publishers.

Macintyre, C. and McVitty K. (2003) *Planning a Pre-5 Setting: An Introduction to Running a Sussessful Nursery*. London: David Fulton Publishers.

Meadows, S. (1993) *The Child as Thinker: The Development and Acquisition of Cognition in Childhood*. London: Routledge.

Miles, E. (1991) 'Auditory dyslexia', in M. Snowling and M. Thomson (eds) *Dyslexia: Integrating Theory and Practice*. London: Whurr Publishers.

Mittler, P. (2000) 'Journeys in inclusive education: profiles and reflections', in P. Clough and J. Corbett (eds) *Theories of Inclusive Education*. London: Sage Publications.

Munden, A. and Arcelus, J. (1999) *The AD/HD Handbook*. London: Jessica Kingsley Publishers.

Nicolson, R.I. and Fawcett, A.J. (1996)*The Dyslexia Early Screening Test (DEST)*. London: The Psychological Corporation.

Piaget, J. (1954) *The Construction of Reality in the Child*. New York: Basic Books.

Pope, M. (1988) 'Dyspraxia – a head teacher's perspective', in *Praxis makes Perfect*. Hitchin: The Dyspraxia Trust.

Portwood, M. (2000) *Developmental Dyspraxia* (second edn) London: David Fulton Publishers.

Portwood, M. (2002) *Using 'a Flying start' – the Durham Baseline Assessment to Identify Youngsters with Special Educational Needs*. Durham: Durham County Council.

Richardson, A. (2000) 'Dyslexia, dyspraxia and ADHD. Can nutrition help?'. Paper presented at the Durham Conference on Dyspraxia, Durham University.

Robinson, N. (1996) 'Role of the speech therapist', in G. Reid (ed) *Dimensions of Dyslexia, Vol. 2, Literacy, Language and Learning.* Edinburgh: Moray House Institute of Education.

Scottish Consultative Council on the Curriculum (1993) *Support for Learning.* SCCC.

Scottish Executive (2002) 'Raising attainment of pupils with special educational needs', *Interchange*, 67: 5.

Scottish Office Education Department (n.d.) *Special Educational Needs Within the 5–14 Curriculum; Support for Learning.* Dundee: SCCC.

Singleton, C.H. (1995) *Cognitive Profiling System (CoPS)*, devised by the Humberside Early Screening research project, University of Hull.

Stein, J. (2000) 'The magnocellular theory of developmental dyslexia', *Dyslexia*, 7: 12–36.

Steinbach, I. (1994) 'How does sound therapy work?'. Paper presented at the 6th European Conference of Neuro-developmental Delay in Children with Specific Learning Difficulties, Klangstudio Lambdoma, Markgrafenufer 9, 59071 Hamm, Germany.

Stewart, R.A. (2002) 'Enabling children with Asperger's syndrome to pretend'. Unpublished masters thesis, University of Edinburgh.

Thomas, A. and Chess, S. (1977) *Temperament and Development.* New York: Brunner/Mazel.

Trevarthen, C. (1997) *Play for Tomorrow.* Video presentation, Edinburgh University.

Vygotsky, L.S. (1978) *Mind and Society.* Cambridge, MA: Harvard University Press.

Wing, L. and Gould, J. (1979) 'Severe impairments of social interaction and associated abnormalities: epidemiology and classification', *Journal of Austism and Developmental Disorders*, 9: 11–29.

# Index